D1591572

The Danish Texans

John L. Davis

The University of Texas
Institute
of Texan
Cultures
at San Antonio

60068

THE TEXIANS AND THE TEXANS

A series dealing with the many kinds of people who have contributed to the history and heritage of Texas.

Now in print:

Pamphlet series: *The Indian Texans, The German Texans, The Norwegian Texans, The Mexican Texans* (in English), *Los Tejanos Mexicanos* (in Spanish), *The Spanish Texans, The Polish Texans, The Greek Texans, The Jewish Texans, The Syrian and Lebanese Texans, The Afro-American Texans, The Anglo-American Texans, The Belgian Texans, The Swiss Texans, The Czech Texans, The French Texans, The Italian Texans* and *The Chinese Texans.*

Book series: *The Danish Texans*
The Irish Texans

The Danish Texans

Copyright 1979
The University of Texas Institute of Texan Cultures at San Antonio

Jack R. Maguire, Executive Director
Pat Maguire, Director of Publications and Coordinator of Programs

Design & Illustration by John E. Johnson

Library of Congress Catalog Number 79-63226
International Standard Book Number 0-933164-56-4 (cloth)
International Standard Book Number 0-933164-57-2 (paper)

This publication was made possible, in part, by a grant from The Houston Endowment, Inc.

Printed in the United States of America

Preface

This book presents the general story of Danish immigration to Texas, showing the major areas of settlement and giving an outline of why these individuals and groups came and what they did after their move. It is a book of good examples, not an exhaustive history. Neither is this work a genealogical reference nor does it presume to tell the story of every Dane who came to Texas. There are far too many individuals for a work of this length.

Most examples included are either first generation arrivals or immediate descendants. Most of them stayed, a few moved on, but all left their mark as part of Texas's diverse culture.

The Danish Texans

Contents

I.
The Danish Texans

The people of Lynchburg decided to take action. Lynchburg was a tiny settlement and ferry crossing where Buffalo Bayou enters the San Jacinto River in present Harris County. It was the end of summer, 1835. William Scott, a former Kentuckian and now a member of Austin's Texas colony, had just offered to equip anyone willing to fight for the cause of Texas against Mexico. The equipping included a good horse with saddle and bridle, a gun and a suit of clothes. Scott was very patriotic and obviously wealthy.

The offer was a straightforward one; the cause of Texas was complex. For several years, Texas settlers, both those from Mexico and the more numerous crowd from the United States, had gotten into difficulties with the Mexican government. Many of the settlers did not like the governmental shift from a states' rights position to central government control less responsive to the far flung colonies. The Anglos from the United States, invited in as settlers, were not familiar with Mexican law or custom, language or religion. Because they had been drawn as immigrants by the almost free land in Mexican Texas, their loyalty to the Mexican government was questionable. Yet at the beginning of real trouble in the 1830's, the settlers seemed merely to want Texas to stand as a separate state, with its own local government, in a Mexican republic.

But there had been clashes. At Anahuac, settlers led by William Barrett Travis, a South Carolina lawyer who had come to Texas to avoid an unhappy marriage, had attacked Mexican troops because of a dispute involving land titles. Trouble simmered, and the Mexican President, Antonio Lopez de Santa

1

Anna, sent troops to the province of Texas to help collect taxes, import duties and to control the colonists. Santa Anna stated that Mexico was not quite ready for democracy.

It didn't work. The Mexican troops were repulsed. About this time, Stephen F. Austin, the Anglo colonial leader, went to Mexico to ask for local self-government. Suspected of supporting Texas insurrection, he was arrested. Released after a year in prison, he returned to Texas converted from the peace-party into a war-party man. The talk in Texas turned to a war for independence, and offers like William Scott's added to the feeling.

About 30 men accepted Scott's offer. Among them was Charles Zanco, a 28-year old Dane who was in the area at the time for a reason now unknown. He was a painter and was probably seeking adventure.

One morning while military business was underway in Lynchburg, Scott, who had been elected captain, approached his second lieutenant, James McGahey, with four yards of blue silk.

"Mac," Scott said, "if you'll make a staff, we'll have a flag."

McGahey did more. First he got Fanny Lynch, the wife of Nathaniel, who not only ran the local ferry but had given his name to the settlement, to reinforce the cloth with a piece of cotton domestic. Then he asked Zanco to paint a design on the flag. Zanco painted a large, five-pointed star in the center.

"Well now," Zanco said, stepping back, "that looks naked. Let me paint something under it. What shall it be?"

McGahey suggested the word "Independence," and Texas soon had a revolutionary flag. The design proved almost too revolutionary. A few settlers passing through to San Felipe thought the design was fine. They took word of the flag to another volunteer group up the bayou at Harrisburg. Like some Texans of the time, the Harrisburg group was ready for action—but not full independence. They made the offer, by courier, to go downstream and shoot any man who raised such a motto before the proper authorities had decided upon such strong action.

The Lynchburg company sent back their own courier politely inviting the Harrisburg men to visit the next day for the flag raising.

When the Lynchburg men raised their flag, two boats of armed men from Harrisburg had pulled up to the bank of the San Jacinto to watch. The flag was unfurled with a flourish and, for a while, no one said a word.

It was a tense moment, but the word "Independence" unfurled in the breeze won everyone over. The two Harrisburg boats pushed off for home. The captain of one stood up, waved his hat, and cried, "Hurrah for the Lone Star!" And locally, that was the start of the revolution.

But not the finish. Charles Zanco left with the group from Lynchburg, going west and into the regular Texas army. He ended up at the Alamo in time to die there five months later.

About the same time Zanco was painting his flag, Christian Hillebrandt, in east Texas, was wondering what to do with his cattle during what looked like the start of a revolution.

Hillebrandt was born around 1800 in Denmark's Schleswig-Holstein area and was an early immigrant to America. He arrived in Louisiana in 1820, married a French-Acadian wife, Eurasie Blanchette, and started ranching.

About 1830, Hillebrandt decided to move to Texas and drove his small herd of cattle across the Louisiana border. Settling in what is now Jefferson County, Hillebrandt filed for and received a league of land in August of 1835.

Hillebrandt may have worried about the impending war, but he weathered those troubled times and many another year. By 1840, he owned 21,000 acres of land, 36 horses and 775 head of cattle—large holdings for those days. At the time of his death in 1858, Hillebrandt's holdings included 9,000 head of cattle, 1,100 horses, 13 slaves and land that included some 1,500 acres near the present site of Beaumont.

Hillebrandt was a very successful businessman for that day, or any time, and established holdings that passed on to descendants. Zanco's contribution

Christian Hillebrandt and his family combine a cattle drive and a move into Texas in 1830

was of the different sort that also goes with settlement and conquest. Both men were Danes, having come a third of the way around the world to cast their fortunes in a new land. Why?

Emigration was not always an accepted thing—from Europe or anywhere else. In earlier years, in many places, it had been illegal. The wealth of a country lay not only in land and money, but in people—people to work and fight. For someone to leave a homeland was more than an insult to the king or parliament—it was an economic loss. But of the curiosity of people there is no end. Add to this personal economic troubles, lack of food, an unstable government, religious persecution, a border or ocean that can be crossed, and emigration starts. Not all these reasons for moving existed in Denmark, or in any one country of Europe, but enough reasons did exist.

Danes coming to the Americas for some of these reasons were eventually to number over 300,000, a small share of which came to Texas. And the story started about the time of Zanco and Hillebrandt.

Amarillo
Happy
Tulia
Lubbock

Red River

El Paso

Colorado River

Ft. Worth
Dallas
Kristenstad

Sabine River

Nacogdoches

Brazos River

Trinity River

Pecos River

Fredericksburg
Stonewall

Hutto
Austin
Bastrop

Lexington

San Jacinto River

Washington-On-
The-Brazos

Beaumont
Lynchburg
Houston
Harrisburg
Anahuac
Galveston

San Antonio

Danevang

TEXAS

Guadalupe River

Rio Grande

Nueces River

Beeville

Indianola

St. Joseph's
Island

100   200

APPROXIMATE SCALE (MILES)

Laredo

Corpus Christi

Hebbronville

McAllen
Brownsville

Areas and Cities of Danish Settlement in Texas

II.
The Start of
Emigration

Denmark is a small, low lying peninsula and some 500 islands on the north side of Germany, dividing the Baltic and North Seas. The most southern of the Scandinavian countries, it has had close relationships, good and bad over the years, with its larger neighbors.

The land is in a central position in northern Europe. In the first millennium A.D., it included part of the homeland of the Anglo-Saxons and lay between the Frisians, Norwegians, Swedes, Germans and British. It soon became a cross-roads of trade in an area of changing empires. Partially as a result, the Danish people are of mixed Nordic stock.

The country came into existence as a national entity over a thousand years ago and at various stages of its history included most of present day Scandinavia as well as overseas colonial holdings. In the days of the Vikings, late in the 9th and the 10th centuries, Denmark even colonized and ruled much of England.

As in most countries, former years were not always pleasant. European troubles were to tie together lands as different as another crossroads called Texas: the Jylland peninsula and 482 islands, the larger of which are Sjaelland, Fyn, Lolland and Falster.

However far ranging as the Vikings were—and there is evidence they knew the Gulf of Mexico—few Danish individuals settled in the Americas, with the exception of the 17th and 18th century Caribbean settlements, before the 19th century. Formerly, even more than today, a country's wealth was measured in

7

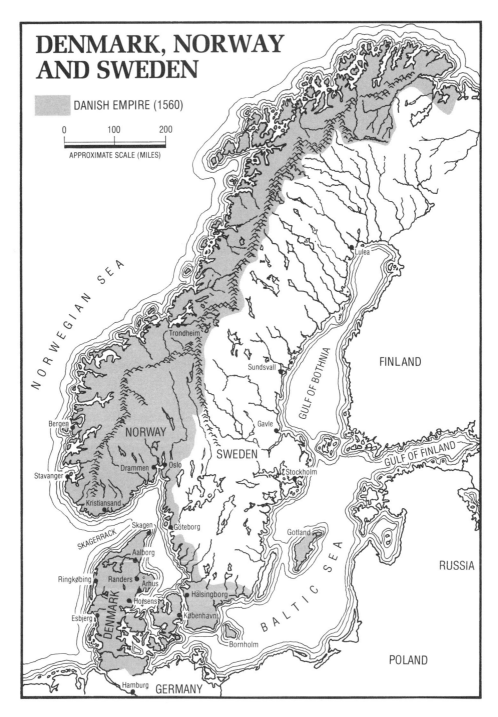

DENMARK, NORWAY AND SWEDEN

DANISH EMPIRE (1560)

0   100   200

APPROXIMATE SCALE (MILES)

NORWEGIAN SEA

Lulea

Trondheim

Sundsvall

GULF OF BOTHNIA

FINLAND

Bergen

NORWAY

Gavle

SWEDEN

Stavanger

Drammen   Oslo

Stockholm

GULF OF FINLAND

Kristiansand

Skagen   Göteborg

Gotland

SKAGERRACK

Aalborg

RUSSIA

Ringkøbing   Randers

Arhus

BALTIC SEA

Horsens

Hälsingborg

Esbjerg

DENMARK

København

Bornholm

POLAND

Hamburg   GERMANY

8

people as well as lands and money. Colonies as part of a national empire might be started, but emigration from one country to another either was not encouraged or was illegal.

In the 1750's, the King of Denmark, Frederick V, warned his people not to listen to the "seductions" of those who would talk of leaving the country. A century later, education for everyone was more common in Europe and so were social revolution and economic depression; emigration was not only permitted, but at times encouraged.

The opening of the Americas created a tremendous frontier which was to absorb some 35 million of Europe's people. Land across the Atlantic would create an escape for many a person caught in the problems of the Old World.

Some individual Danes left their homeland in early years, but the bulk of the emigration occurred between 1820 and 1920.

Denmark in the 19th century was a country undergoing change. After many centuries, the status of the small farmer and the hired worker had declined. Taxes increased and land was often taken up in large holdings, a legacy of the 13th through 16th centuries. In some areas of Denmark, until the late 18th century, it was illegal for farm workers to leave the estate on which they were born. The government and large landholders believed they had to tie people to the land as workers, or the economy would fail.

In addition, the 19th century brought better health and medical care. In former centuries, a sizeable percentage of those born died as infants, and a person's life was none too long. With improved medical care, the birth rate increased and the death rate decreased. In many areas, this meant serious over-population.

A farmer's meal in Denmark, 1860

Danish fishermen, 1860

Laws were changed. Young men were no longer bound to work for estate owners, but there was little land for them to buy in the country, even if they had money, and few jobs in town. The common man was most often a poor man.

People coming of age, marrying and starting families simply could not earn a living. In the 1870's, a farmhand's pay came to about 100 *kroner* a year, but the annual cost of an average laborer's household was over 230 *kroner*. How could one get married? One could not even buy a farm and house without 30 years of saving for just the down payment—even when a good place was available.

In 1801, there were about 962,000 people in Denmark. Somewhat more than a century later, the number would be four times as large, not counting over 300,000 people who would leave the country.

Danes drifted from the countryside into the towns, hoping to become tradesmen or work in the new factories. But there, in the 1870's the industrial revolution was slow in getting started. Even before 1870, when there was no such thing as unemployment pay, the percentage of unemployed in the towns rose to 50%.

Danish women in Slesvig costume, c. 1860

Yet the people were educated. A system of compulsory education—started in 1814 for all children—had given a new generation the power to think for themselves. The possibility of changing things or of simply leaving the country were new realizations. Under the social pressure, it had also become possible. Even the government had no answers. A person could, theoretically, choose his own fate—at least he could leave the country and try life somewhere else.

So the Dane, pressed to make a living, at times drifted from his home town to the city, and from the city across an ocean.

The voyage of *Die Elbe* was one such venture that did not get very far, but did illustrate how much people wanted to come to America. Early accounts hint that the voyage was planned to the Gulf of Mexico region.

In August of 1838, Jacob Dessau of Aarhus ran an advertisement in the local newspaper seeking people to join in a voyage to America. The lands west across the ocean were thought to be places of unlimited opportunity. Really for the first time, people heard news of such places from travelers and in newspapers. Public information was a new and powerful thing.

10

About 60 Danes responded and they set out in their newly-bought, second-hand ship. They sailed right out into a storm in the Kattegat Sea. After reviving their resolve in north Jylland, the group sailed south through the English Channel into an Atlantic storm that drove them into the Bay of Biscay. On the coast of Spain, they found themselves in the midst of a Spanish civil war. They were plundered by pirates, cast ashore, and left, in their words, desolate and without a drop of beer. Some of the Danes made it back home years later.

This group had failed, but the general yearning was not quenched. Some were to try again. In the early 19th century, ship travel was still quite uncertain. As passenger vessels, the ships were primitive and could not carry a lot of people. This was to change but, at first, it was difficult for a group of people to travel together.

Other individual Danes were luckier in their travels, perhaps because they were better sailors. One, Peter Johnson, went to sea as a young man and was soon operating his own vessel, the threemasted *Belleport,* in international trade. For him, leaving the country meant something quite different from the first emigrants.

In 1832, Johnson put into a Gulf of Mexico port, perhaps Mobile, and from that time took up shipping on American coasts. He apparently liked the New World. He became a citizen of the United States and started operating ships between Mobile, New Orleans and Galveston. He was soon bringing settlers and supplies to the Mexican province of Texas.

Engraving of Corpus Christi's port, 1846

Engraving of Galveston, c. 1852

Brownsville and the Santa Cruz Ferry, 1863

11

He liked Texas. At the close of the revolution, Captain Johnson moved his base to Galveston and became a citizen of the Republic. In 1850, he located at Indianola where he became the government mail runner from there to Corpus Christi. This led him further into the coastal shipping business which he successfully operated until the Civil War, both at sea and on land.

Captain Johnson built a large, two-story building at the west end of St. Joseph's Island as a warehouse and home. It was soon the center of a small settlement. By this time, he owned two ships, three landside stage stations and routes, two stagecoaches and a ferry boat. He managed quite a crew of captains, teamsters and freight handlers.

About this time he also married Wilhelmina Rabel, an Alsatian. In fact, he married her twice, once in a civil ceremony at Indianola and later in a church service at the young town of Lamar.

Life in the large building on St. Joseph's Island was pleasant enough until the Civil War when United States forces began a blockade. Federal vessels sailed the coast, putting an end to shipping, and Captain Johnson's business went down hill. Not only did he have to hide his ships, but home life became trying. Gunners of the Federal navy, as they patrolled the coast, used the settlement—and particularly the captain's taller building—for target practice.

*Captain Peter Johnson's family takes shelter as his home on St. Joseph's Island
is used for target practice by United States ships during the Civil War*

12

Finally, harassed by landing parties and the increased accuracy of Union warships, the captain gave up and moved his family inland near Lamar. Shortly after, his house and the little settlement were sacked and burned by United States forces.

The captain and his family weathered the Civil War, but he did not return to the sea. He took up farming, cattle trading and salt selling.

In fact, the captain contacted Union forces after the war and told them that the postal service had been somewhat interrupted by the conflict and they had neglected to reinstate it. He presented a petition to the government about the conditions. The petition was not only granted, but also Captain Johnson was named postmaster at Lamar. His home became the post office, and so it remained until his death in 1895.

Another Dane who became a seafarer was John Edward Henrichson, only about 12 years old when he put to sea as a cabin boy in 1819. He had been working for his father in Copenhagen, learning the cabinetmaking trade. For a while, most of their work was for ships: building the trunks and cabinets, shelves and containers for trading vessels. Young Henrichson liked the work and the ships but was more fascinated by their destinations. The prospect of an exciting voyage lured him.

With the help of a ship captain who was also a family friend, Henrichson convinced his father that he was old enough to leave on a voyage. His age might have been questionable, but his size was not. As an adult, he would stand almost seven feet tall and weigh nearly three hundred pounds of very well developed muscle and bone. At a little past 12 years old, he was as large as most sailors.

The elder Henrichson relented and young John put to sea. He first served as a cabin boy, attending to the officers' meals and making himself generally useful. But the officers soon realized they had a willing volunteer as well as an employee. Henrichson soon was helping with the records of the trading ship and had changed part of his duty to that of a cabinetmaker and repairman aboard ship.

More voyages followed and one part of the world caught the young man's eye —the western coast of the Gulf of Mexico. Matamoros, at the mouth of the Rio Grande, was a frequent port of call and here young Henrichson helped the traders sell cargoes of cheese, lumber and European manufactured goods. At least once when the ship was being cleaned and repaired, Henrichson accompanied the captain and his party to Monterrey and Saltillo, Mexico. Other times, the crew would take flatboats up the Rio Grande, trading with the ranchers upstream. Henrichson saw a lot of the country. He had also learned French, Spanish and English and was a very valuable crew member at bargaining time.

The trading stops also included the first Texas ports: the mouth of the Nueces, at Powderhorn, Copano and Matagorda Bays, Galveston Bay, then to New Orleans.

Henrichson became interested in land around the Nueces River. He heard of the possibilities of obtaining a land grant from the Mexican government, yet apparently never completed a petition.

New Orleans became his first New World home. On one trip there, Henrichson persuaded his captain to leave him in the port to buy sugar, hides and flour for the next trip. The captain agreed. However, in the course of Henrichson's purchases, he drifted out of seafaring.

The plantations of New Orleans in the early 19th century were houses of trade, and Henrichson naturally had to visit them to get the best prices. In addition to purchasing, there was the Louisiana social life to deal with. Balls were often given in the evenings by plantation owners and businessmen were invited. The dances of the French and the Anglo reels and jigs blended during the evenings. But standing an impressive head or two taller at these gatherings was Henrichson, the blond Viking of Danish and Swedish heritage.

At one such gathering, the owner of the plantation, a wealthy widow, caught Henrichson's eye. The effect was mutual. Henrichson visited later to improve his French, next to help sell the products of the sprawling lands, then he remained as husband of the woman and manager of the plantation.

After his marriage, Henrichson continued to travel between New Orleans and the Texas coast with shiploads of wax and sugar and manufactured goods in return for the products of Texas and Mexico: hides and silver, wool and oils, the dyes cochineal and indigo. On the Louisiana plantation, Henrichson's family managed while he was away; the widow had older children when she married the wandering Norseman. Henrichson and the widow—whose name is not remembered in the family—had three children, two girls and a boy.

In the late 1830's, Henrichson was again attracted to the Nueces-Powderhorn area of Texas. A revolution had come and gone and the land seemed ripe for settling. Henrichson also knew that his wife and her children would never leave Louisiana.

So, with or without her knowledge, he left, taking his children Mary Ellen, Catherine and George Washington. They never returned. In fact, once settled as a rancher and trader in the future Corpus Christi area, Henrichson never used his own name on cargo to and from New Orleans. Thus, he could not be easily traced.

The children were between five and ten years of age when Henrichson arrived, but were a great help. On a frontier, everybody works. He had chosen to come in the summer so good weather would favor their land hunting and

John Edward Henrichson and his three children settle on the Nueces River

house building. After a year or two, they had a substantial ranch somewhat inland near San Patricio largely on the south bank of the Nueces. Henrichson found himself in the "Irish Colonies" founded in the days of Mexican control.

The land was sparsely settled, but the Dane knew that the area would attract more people. He began to buy parcels of land, improve them as ranch holdings and sell them at a good profit. His own ranchlands became well known. He operated a supply store and was soon known as "El Grandor," certainly because of his size and physical prowess, but also because he could speak any local language and was a friend to all.

Henrichson was too large a man to regularly ride the small mustang horses. In fact, when he tried, his feet almost touched the ground and his weight was the equivalent of two men. The nearby Mexican settlers had several humorous phrases for the sight, and Henrichson gave up this mode of transportation. Nor did he particularly like wagons. In walking, however, he excelled: a walk of 10 miles was nothing to the man. His ranch foremen would often have to trot their horses to keep up with him. A man who neither took a drink nor smoked, Henrichson developed great physical endurance.

When the Mexican War started, General Zachary Taylor landed at Corpus Christi Bay with instructions to cross the Nueces River (which Mexico regarded as the Texas border) into the disputed territory north of the Rio Grande. This naturally precipitated hostilities. Henrichson and his young son decided to enlist and go along with the army, apparently mostly for the fun. The father enlisted as a blacksmith and his son as a wagon driver. Soon they were at Fort Brown and, indeed, got their fill of adventure. Young George was narrowly missed by a cannon ball, Henrichson was at the Battle of Resaca de las Palmas, and both spent long days keeping the army horses shod and repairing metal equipment. They had enough of the war in Texas without going farther. As the United States troops marched south across the Rio Grande singing *The Girl I Left Behind Me,* the Henrichsons, at least in family tradition, returned to the Nueces singing, *My Black Eyed Señorita.*

Henrichson apparently never said what he thought about the United States' imperialistic war in which he involved himself, but settled back into his ranching business. He became a rather rich man, as far as anyone knows. Distrusting banks, he converted his wealth, the proceeds of cattle and land sales, into gold coin and buried it somewhat on his lands. He was successful enough in business to leave the bulk of it in the ground. The gold was still buried in 1877, when his son George was summoned home from a cattle shipping trip to be present at his father's death.

When George entered his father's room, the elder man waved him over to the bed. Henrichson had caught pneumonia and was struggling to breathe. He could hardly talk.

Henrichson tried to tell his son where the gold had been buried, indicating that corral posts were connected in some way with the site or sites. But his voice broke, for a moment he fought for breath, then died. Neither George nor any other member of the family ever found the hiding place of the gold.

But the ranch lands themselves supported the family, and several to come. George Washington Henrichson lived to start a large local family with his wife Elizabeth Charlotte Ashton. A slender man with sandy hair and blue eyes—a mixture of the French and the Northmen—he was as well known as his father.

John is buried at the old cemetery at San Patricio, George at Sandia, but the family, comprising many members, lives on.

III.
A Few
Individuals

Danes who came to Texas in the 1850's and 1860's, including those from other parts of the United States, had survived a perilous ocean voyage. They then entered the state either overland, often from the plains of the midwest, or by ship along the Gulf Coast.

Only the United States' Civil War slowed the traffic for a few years. The frontier remained open, however; and as soon as the conflict was settled, even more Europeans lined up to come. The perils of the Atlantic voyage, particularly before the 1870's, were considerable. As emigration from Europe increased, ship owners and captains were quick to capitalize on this desire to cross the ocean. Some were unscrupulous, crowding passengers into filthy holds formerly used only for cargo. At times, more than 800 passengers were lodged between decks, subject to the most horrible stages of seasickness, unable to eat for days. Aboard ship, inadequate food, poor or lacking sanitary facilities and even a brutal crew were not uncommon. Death was frequent on the Atlantic voyage. Cholera and measles would occasionally decimate those aboard. Once at sea, there was no escape.

Some Atlantic passages were more humane, even pleasant—on a good ship in favorable weather with adequate food and sleeping quarters. Yet the voyage was tedious at best. After 1900, the sailing time across the Atlantic would be cut to two weeks, but in mid-19th century, steamships were not common and the trip was slow. Depending on the weather, the voyage could take from about 35 to 60 days. And this was the time between the common transfer point,

Liverpool, England, and New York, not the whole journey.

In Denmark, unrest was reaching high levels. Religious groups gathered not only to save souls but also to emigrate to America. The Church of Jesus Christ of Latter-day Saints, the Mormon Church, was particularly active in missionary work—and arranging for the emigration of converts to the United States. Few of these families, however, came directly to Texas. Denmark's defeat by Germany in the War of 1864, and the disastrous peace treaty which followed, not only lost all of Schleswig and Holstein, but also many a citizen who chose to try his fortune elsewhere.

Danes at home, considering the possibilities of emigration in the 1850's

Burial of an emigrant child at sea, 1882

Emigrants at dinner aboard ship, 1840's

The first of the travel agents offered tickets to the New World, for a fee, and some former emigrants even came back for a visit to Denmark, usually bearing good stories of life overseas. The government openly approved of emigration.

Danish emigrants were beginning to show up in Texas. In the 1850 census, Danes were counted in at least ten counties: Tarrant, Ft. Bend, Bexar, Galveston, Liberty, Matagorda, Nacogdoches and—most of all—in the counties of the lower Rio Grande Valley. There were only about 50 Danes listed, but they represented a wide range of employment. Otto Kass was a soldier at Ft. Worth; Thomas Moosewood was a wagon master for the military in Bexar County; William Davisson and Peter Hansen were seamen at Galveston; D. B. Leoz was a clerk, Peter Miller a carpenter, and Christian Bedstrup a boatman, all in the Valley. They had survived the long journey to enter a new life.

In the late 1840's, George Henry Trube and his wife Sophie Dorothea Knute of the harbor of Kiel, a German possession after 1864, decided to come to America. Trube had been a gardener for a nobleman, and with three sons, decided to cast his fortune elsewhere.

Charles Frederick Trube   *Henry John Trube*   *John Clement Trube*

John Clement Trube, one of the sons, was 10 when the family arrived on the east coast. Some years later, John left home, drifted to the Gulf area, and found a job as cabin boy on the steamer *Farmer* between Galveston and Houston. He liked the area. By 1855, John had started a real estate business in Houston and two years later had married Veronica Durst, a daughter of a Swiss family. In fact, the families became closely related. John's brother Henry John Trube married Sophia Durst in 1857, settled himself in the area, and the other brother, Charles Frederick Trube, married Henrietta Bock, a half-sister in the Durst family.

The brothers set up their respective businesses and investments. Charles set up a shop repairing watches and ship's instruments. John Clement Trube moved to Galveston in 1868 after serving in the Civil War. There, he built up a chain of investments that, in four years, when he was 35, allowed him to retire.

In 1890, however, John Clement decided to build a new home. Doing most of the design himself—family members later said he fondly remembered details from a Danish castle—Trube entered into a $9700 contract with John W. Pope, contractor, and Alfred Muller, architect. Money went a long way before the turn of the century. The result was a 30-room mansion that is a historical landmark today.

Trube home, Galveston

Stairway of the Trube home, Galveston   *Bedroom in the Trube home, Galveston*

The home was described by an architectural critic a few years ago as a "fearless melange," possessing an "exuberant spirit." Another called it an "undisciplined and individualistic cross between Gothic and Moorish design." The home is certainly unique. The building is brick, plastered with Belgian cement to resemble cut stone. The mansard roof is slated with 12 gables, and an unusual, ornate chimney divides as it rises to frame a cathedral window with stained glass imported from Italy. Despite all this the home took only three months to build.

More important than some details, the building has survived many a hurricane in Galveston with no more damage than a few bits of fallen plaster. John Clement Trube died in 1925, but the house is still in the family, still as solid as ever.

One Dane who apparently never stated a reason for coming to America was Christian Dorbrandt who arrived in 1834. Born in Denmark in 1818, he was 16 when he arrived but apparently did not come to avoid military service. Dorbrandt joined the United States army and fought as a private in the Mexican War.

The young man then decided to stay with the army and was first stationed in Maryland. On a visit to New Orleans in the early 1850's, he met and married Annie Dunlavy of Ireland who was visiting her uncle.

Dorbrandt was transferred to Ft. Sill, Indian Territory, then to Ft. Croghan near Burnet, Texas. He served as quartermaster sergeant there for a while, but with the closing of the fort in 1855, Dorbrandt retired from the army and built a home near present Marble Falls. Here, the young couple's first child, a daughter named Henrietta, was born. She was the first of 14 children who were to form a large central Texas family.

An Indian group on the move, 1870   *Drawing of an Indian raid, 1873*

Dorbrandt did not have the military out of his blood, however, and served as a Texas Ranger captain, then joined the Confederate army. Often during the Civil War, Annie was left alone in their rock home in Backbone Valley. More than once, she locked herself in and kept armed guard over her children while Indians threatened.

Dorbrandt, at 60 years of age, patrolled the Colorado River area around Austin with the Rangers as they made the transition from Indian fighters to lawmen. Dorbrandt and his wife also built and operated a gin after a later move to the South Gabriel community. He led an active life and died in 1910.

The Dane remained rather a military man all his life. One grandson recalled how all the children's shoes (and those of three grandchildren who lived in the home) had to be cleaned, polished and lined up in precise order for the next morning. The grandchild assumed this was a carry-over from his grandfather's army days. It might also have been a necessity with, at any one time, at least a dozen people to get up and off to school.

One son, Christian Jr., was a cattle trail rider for years and became city marshal of Burnet and sheriff of the county before he went into ranching as a full time profession.

Not all Danes who came to America were from the middle and lower classes, workmen and farmers. Baron de Løvenskiold made the same decision.

The Løvenskiold family was a prominent one in Denmark. It included relations to Norwegian families dating back to when most of that country was part of the Danish empire. Individuals of high government rank and accomplished literary and scientific talents were common.

Charles Grimur Thorkelin Løvenskiold was born in 1823 at Kronborg Castle, at Elsinore. Here, where the young man's family was in the service of the king, he was surrounded by the opulence of royalty: paintings, music, weapons of the Norsemen and the sagas of his forefathers. Educated by private tutors, then at the University of Copenhagen, Løvenskiold became a master linguist, knowing French, Greek, Latin, German, Spanish, Italian, English and, of course, Danish. He also learned Danish court law and received superb military training.

When he was 19, a new world beckoned. He set sail for New York, remaining there a time before sailing down to Florida, then to New Orleans. Here, the young baron was commissioned as a lieutenant because of his past military training. In the city, he met Sophie, the daughter of Sarah and Joseph Clark. They were married in 1848 and in New Orleans a son, Oscar, was born. Here also, the young baron dropped his royal titles, and the "ø" in his name changed to "o" in the New World.

In New Orleans in the 1850's, there was much talk of the new state of Texas. Colonel Henry Lawrence Kinney, a promoter and developer, interested the young man in his calls for settlement on the coast. Lovenskiold decided on Corpus Christi, and in 1853 the family settled in their new home.

In 1855, Lovenskiold decided to open an academy for young men and women. He brought in a faculty of three teachers and started Corpus Christi Academy. The school flourished and attracted students from Texas and Mexico.

After a while, Lovenskiold sold the school but kept busy practicing law. He became known as a powerful speaker who could hold his own in any courtroom.

At the outbreak of the Civil War, he became a colonel for the Confederacy. During the war, and at the close of hostilities when he was a prisoner, the colonel's health was injured. A severe bronchial infection, later requiring surgery, caused him virtually to lose his voice. This curtailed his speaking in court but not his activity. He merely joined up with a "speaking partner," and the law firm went on.

After the war, in 1867, a yellow fever epidemic struck the city. The Lovenskiold family cooked meals and the colonel took the food to needy families. In the evenings, the children were kept awake by the hammering of coffin makers who worked across the street from the Lovenskiold's home at Blucher and Carancahua Streets . . . but the family escaped the plague.

Point Isabel, Texas, 1846

Capture of the Federal gunboat Harriet Lane during the Confederate attack retaking Galveston, January 1863

Confederate naval attack during the capture of Galveston, January 1, 1863

Confederate attack on Galveston, January 1863

The Galveston waterfront, 1855

Lovenskiold's law practice, with businesses as well as individuals, was a success and he became well known in south Texas. He became a frequently elected alderman of the city and was so serving at his death in 1875. Two sons, Oscar and Perry, were mayors of Corpus Christi.

The Danes in early Texas, the Lovenskiolds, Trubes, Zanco, Bedstrup and others, were few compared to other groups of immigrants. They brought intelligence and daring, resourcefulness and skills. They made a direct contribution to Texas, but they did not transplant a culture. They came as individuals. In the years before the peak of emigration near the turn of the century, this would remain the case. Danish colonial efforts were still to come.

IV.
Lee County:
"Little Denmark"

Sometime in the 1860's—the exact year is now forgotten—two Texans turned up in Denmark asking if anyone wanted to move to central Texas. This rather unlikely question, however, fell upon receptive ears.

The two men were Travis Shaw and John Hester, and the main reason for their trip was probably to sell land. Shaw lived near Lexington on land his father had received for Texas revolutionary military service, and Hester was a German whose wife, Louise Larsen, was Danish. She had come to Texas earlier with three brothers. Perhaps it was Louise who influenced the trip to Europe.

Today, it is no longer known just which families came directly from Denmark and which families moved from other places in the United States, but within a few years, north Lee County was known as "Little Denmark."

In the 1860's, the area was Burleson County. Lee County was created in 1874 largely from Burleson and Bastrop Counties. It was a pleasant plain of open fields separated by swaths of post oak. The oldest settlement anywhere around was Lexington, which had been settled in the 1850's.

Initially, over 20 Danish families came to the area about eight miles west of Lexington, and others moved in between 1870 and 1880. A few continued to arrive until about the turn of the century. Most of the Danes who chose this area for a new home were farmers or farm workers, but a few were craftsmen in various trades.

Christian Moelbeck, a saddlemaker, his wife, her brother and a related family, Mr. and Mrs. C. D. A. Schutt, were among the first to arrive. Paul Paulsen was a cabinetmaker; Niels Thompson was a carpenter and bricklayer; Klaus and Jens Thomassen were farmers; and Peter Jensen was a blacksmith. Other families were led by Hans Sorensen, Peter Andersen, Neils Petersen, Niels Christian Olsen, Peter Nygaard, Rasmus Rasmussen, Jacob Vittrup and a host of others. Some single men arrived; most married local girls. Some husbands came from Denmark alone, to send for their family later as they established themselves.

On board an emigrant ship, 1870

Immigrants picking up train tickets in New York on the way west, 1880

Here were enough families to preserve things Danish—for a short time. Most of the families adapted quickly to American life. After all, in their new home, they were a very small minority. Names changed: Thomassen became Thompson, Højst became Hoyst, Rasmussen changed to Robertson and Jens became Yens as a Dane gave up trying to write the "J" for Americans who pronounced it another way.

This change in spelling happened to many a Danish name in the Americas. Some Danish individuals adopted German spelling, some Norwegian or Swedish, and some took what they thought was "American."

For centuries, the Danes had used patronymic names: The son would be called by his father's name plus "-son," or "-sen" in Danish. This resulted in a family name changed with each generation. In 1856, a government decree abolished the system. Family names were fixed, leaving even one-third of the population with "-sen" endings. This spelling was often changed to "-son" in the United States.

There were other changes. A few families in the Lee County area taught their children Danish, but this did not last for long. Members drifted out of the Lutheran church to join local denominations. Church gatherings were considerably different in this new land, particularly the brush arbor gatherings or camp meetings. Near the Hvidberg farm, Brother Henry Purser, a Methodist minister, conducted his outdoor meeting. Families arrived ready to camp out for up to a week. They brought chicken coops on their wagons or even led milk cows. In the days before ice, food had to be transported fresh. The wagons also carried blankets for sleeping, some even a tent. In a week's time, Brother Purser, or men like him, could count on quite a few conversions. And some Danish families were at the camp meetings.

The Danes enjoyed visiting among themselves, and there was a lasting community spirit. They did not give up their family gatherings that, besides beer and polkas, now included new found dominoes. They did not give up their kartofler (boiled potatoes) or rodgrod (a thickened, fruit juice pudding) at mealtimes. Nor did they often forget the custom of pastry and coffee every day at 10 a.m. and at 3 p.m.—a requirement if visitors were in the home.

But most of the Danes did what other early settlers had to do: the women made clothes for the family, prepared the food and took care of the young children while the men farmed or worked at a craft, more often *and* worked at a craft, selling any surplus in town.

Jens Thomassen's story is not uncommon. He and his brother Klaus were sons of a parish school teacher who lived on the North Sea side of Jylland near Thisted. Emigration from this part of Denmark would reach 89 people out of 1000. Talk about going elsewhere was in the air.

Jens and Klaus Thomassen arrive in Lee County, 1874

27

In 1870, the brothers decided to make their move. Jens was 21 when he arrived in New York, unable to speak English, but aware that other Danes he traveled with were going to Chicago. There, he was a quarry worker for awhile, but decided to leave for Louisiana. It was no better. Cutting barrel staves from cypress logs in a mosquito-infested bayou country was not to his liking. In 1874, he and his brother heard of, then came to, Lee County. Jens Thomassen, now Yens Thompson, was attracted by more than the farmland. He met and married Anna Oman, a Swedish girl who lived there.

Four boys and four girls were born to the young couple. Yet, Lee County was a frontier, and these were years well before antibiotics and regular medical care. Food and shelter were not the only problems. Two boys died as children, and their mother died of pneumonia in 1894.

Yens later married a widow, Mrs. Denolus Thomas, a school teacher known as Nolie. Yens and Nolie had three daughters born to them and also reared Nolie's daughter by her former marriage. It was a large group. Years later, a younger daughter, Flora Thompson, wrote of the family: "None of us had ever 'set the world on fire.' We just 'growed' on a sandhill farm three miles west of Lexington, the whole 'pahsel' of us." Six children of the family were teachers, and a son, Thomas W. Thompson, became county attorney, then county judge.

This family, like most of the others, produced leading citizens, farmed and built, and solved the problems of living very much like families today. An immigrant is merely a person with a new home. In fact, most of the problems are the same: how to make a living, raise a family, make a chair or a poem or a good corn crop and find joy in life.

The Danes of north Lee County seemed to do just that. Most families raised large vegetable gardens along with orchards of fruit trees. Niels Thompson operated Thompson's Gin for cotton in the Liberty settlement area and made bricks; and Peter Christian Jensen, originally from Copenhagen, soon had what he could not have in Denmark—a farm of 375 acres. After a dispute about who could attend a local private school, Peter gave part of his land for a school which he named the "Equal Rights School" because anyone could attend.

Some of the first arrivals moved on after a number of years to Williamson County or Rockdale or Austin—as did most of their children.

Today, the original Danish families are hard to spot through their descendants. There were not enough people to form a lasting colony, and acculturation of local habits and intermarriage evened out the differences. Yet asking about the Danes in Lee County today usually brings forth a simple response: "They're mighty fine people."

V.
Increased Emigration: Families and Groups

The peak years of Danish emigration lay between 1885 and about 1895. National legislation had required ship companies to provide better facilities for passengers, the new steamships had cut the Atlantic passage time to between 11 and 14 days, and emigration agents thronged Europe selling tickets to America. Books and brochures described not only the general desirability of America, but also listed specific areas where land or jobs were available. And most letters from relatives in America confirmed the opportunities.

In the earlier groups of Danish emigrants, the percentage of single men was slightly higher. By the turn of the century, the number of children declined to half what it had been as family size declined generally in Denmark and more young couples emigrated on their own. In 1870, about 50% of the Danish emigrants were in family groups. By 1890, only 25% were families. The motive for emigration began to change from a hard economic necessity to a desire for adventure, of fortune hunting. Few of the emigrants were starving, but most thought they could better their lot in life elsewhere. When asked why they emigrated, most people answered "I did not want to be a common laborer in my own country" or "I did not care to live such a life of drudgery and poverty as my parents lived; I can't do worse in America, and I may do better."

And America was getting the best people. Some countries, including Denmark, did rouse the ire of American officials by occasionally shipping out criminals on the next boat. But the practice was rare. Careful studies made in some areas—particularly Sweden—show that the average Scandinavian emi-

Emigrants boarding a steamer
in Hamburg, Germany, 1894

The hold of an emigrant ship, 1869

Emigrants in the ship's steerage, 1905

Interior of an immigrant train, 1874

Emigrants below decks on a steamer, 1860's

An immigrant train going west, 1880's

grant setting out for the New World was measurably more intelligent, had a better education, and was a bit more enterprising than the person of the same social class that stayed at home. America was not a dumping ground, except in an economic sense. It received the flower of Europe's people.

Most of those who came from Denmark did not own land. They were farm workers, servants, and younger sons and daughters. A few, about 3%, were land holders; fishermen accounted for nearly 2%; businessmen and professionals totaled almost 8%; some 18% were craftsmen and apprentices; about 25% were domestic or industrial workers from town; and almost 44% were rural laborers, the landless.

Dealing with these people were the emigration agents. Independent or in the pay of transportation or land companies, they set up headquarters in towns and toured the countryside. They sold ship tickets, railroad tickets for the land part of the journey in America, guidebooks and even supplies for the voyage.

Sometimes, even though traveling conditions were improving, emigrants were handled like cattle. The American Aid & Homestead Company, while recruiting emigrants, claimed to have vast Texas holdings. When the company suddenly admitted bankruptcy, one boatload of 400 Scandinavians was actually auctioned off. Officials of the Southern Pacific Railroad, who wanted settlers to buy their land, bought rights to the entire group for a commission of $5000. Some emigrants, unable to speak English and generally confused over the arrangements, ended up where they had no plans to be. "Runners" or baggage grabbers thronged ports, officially charging little for helping the newly arrived immigrant with luggage and information, but many were swindlers and confidence men. The worst were perfectly capable of separating the newly arrived person from most of his money.

Travel agents from Texas, Arkansas and California set up shop in Copenhagen and engaged in highly competitive campaigns to secure emigrants, just a little short of shanghaiing, in the opinion of some observers. C. D. Friedel, an agent from the Cunard Ship Line, was himself a Danish brewer who immigrated to Texas, then returned to work as an agent in Copenhagen. The second move was probably more profitable.

But all of the perils were braved, most emigrants survived, and the Danes arrived in increasing numbers. No one knows just how many Danes decided that the New World was not for them and went home. Some studies show this number may have been as high as 10% from some areas.

The Danes were a bit different from the Norwegians or Swedes. More Danes went to other parts of the world (particularly Australia), and a greater percentage than other Scandinavians was men. The Danes sent back only about one-half as many prepaid tickets to America as the Norwegians. Immigration statistics hint that the Danes were a bit more individualistic in their choices of direction of travel and where to live. Still, 88% of the emigrating Danes came to America. Of all the Scandinavians, they spread out more over the country, did not congregate into communities as much, and were the most quickly assimilated into the American way of life.

For the 1840-1914 period, about 309,000 Danes left their homeland, compared to 1,105,000 Norwegians and about 754,000 Swedes. The emigration rate itself, the percentage, was almost always lower in Denmark.

Danes who came to Texas in the latter three decades of the 19th century had often seen considerable travel before they settled down.

One such was John J. Peez, later Captain John Peetz, after a slight name change. He was born in Schleswig and came with his parents John and Annie Peez to New Orleans in 1849. The family moved to Mobile where John J. soon learned the trade of ship's carpenter.

He left on his first voyage just in time to join the British navy and end up in the Crimean War. Leaving that employment, he sailed on successive ships to Peru, Chile, Argentina, Holland, Massachusetts and back to New Orleans.

Working on the Gulf coast, he joined Confederate forces at the start of the Civil War and ended up for a time as an artilleryman, very much on land, in the Appalachians. His occupation was finally realized and he was returned to naval duty.

After the war, and a trip to Europe, Peetz came to Galveston and engaged in coastal trade east to Louisiana and west to Tampico. In 1874, he married Alvena Langholz, also a native of Schleswig, who came to Texas through another coincidence. Her father was Major A. H. Langholz, a Dane serving with Union forces. He had come to Texas with Federal troops during recon-struction and shortly thereafter brought his family to Galveston. Here, the Danish captain met his future wife.

Christian Andersen had a somewhat similar story, but ended up further in-land. Young Christian lived outside Aalborg, Denmark, where his father was a small land holder. Christian's first job, in 1844 when he was five, was tending geese, but by the time he was ten his horizons had broadened. He had heard of the gold fields of California. His mother died when he was 16, his father re-married, and Christian was drafted to fight the Germans. This he did, but Denmark lost. This War of 1864 lost Schleswig and Holstein to Germany until 1920 when north Schleswig was returned to Denmark through a plebiscite, a general vote. For the Danes in these provinces, the decades were confusing. Although Christian did not live in the transferred provinces, he decided to leave Denmark.

In 1866, Christian and a wartime acquaintance, Harry Johnsen, traveled to

DANISH NAMES ON SHIP LISTS TO GALVESTON, 1847-1861:

1. Biel, Carl—Norden; wife Mathilda nee Hander—Christiansfeld, Denmark to Austin County, *Magnet*, 1851.
2. Bobzien, Fried. with wife—Trendelberg, Denmark; *Copernicus*, 1852.
3. Hander, Amalie Maria—Christiansfeld, Denmark to San Antonio; *Gutenberg*, 1855.
4. Hander, Carl—Christiansfeld, Denmark to Fayette Co.; *Gutenberg*, 1855.
5. Hander, Christian Wilhelm—Christiansfeld, Denmark to Austin Co., later to Falls Co.; *Gutenberg*, 1855.
6. Hander, Julius—Christiansfeld, Denmark to Washington Co., later to McLennon Co., *Gutenberg*, 1855.
7. Hander, Maren, 50 (died in Comal Co., 1856), Carl 22, Christian 21, Julius 18, Maria 15, Charlotte 12—Christiansfeld, Denmark; *Gutenberg*, 1855.
8. Hansen, Lorenz—Sunderbord, Denmark; *Copernicus*, 1852.
9. Jessen, Joh. Henrik, 36—Svendborg, Denmark; *Gutenberg*, 1855.
10. Marxen, Phil.—Marne, Denmark; *Copernicus*, 1852.
11. Matsen, Ch.—Oesterbye, Denmark; *Washington*, 1852.
12. Meyer, Christian & wife—Helgoland to Bexar; *Gaston*, 1860.
13. Neils, Hans, 25—Bordesholm, Holstein; *Gutenberg*, 1855.
14. Nicolaisen, Nils—Oesterbye, Denmark; *Washington*, 1852.
15. Niedermann, Carl—Middelfarth, Denmark; *Washington*, 1852.
16. Nielsen, Cornel—Röming, Denmark; *Washington*, 1852.
17. Plambeck, Heinrich, Catharina, Christian, Heinrich, Anna, Catharina—Newmuenster, Holstein; *Gutenberg*, 1855.
18. Schnoor, Claus, wife & 4 children—Kuden, Denmark; *Copernicus*, 1852.
19. Schnoor, Heinrich, wife & 8 children—*Copernicus*, 1852.
20. Steffansen, Caroline 16 with Joh. H. Jessen—Svendborg, Denmark; *Gutenberg*, 1855.
21. Stein, Christian, Doris, Hein., Christian, Hans—Neumuenster, Holstein; *Gutenberg*, 1855.
22. Staertjer, Anna—Garz, Holstein; *Hampden*, 1854.
23. Striegler, J. F. G. 41, Christine 41, Ernestine 18, Alphorstine 16, Arthur 15, Wilhelm 13, Nicolaus 12, Ida 11, Friedr. 7, Olga 4, Jens ¼,—Svendborg, Denmark to Gillespie Co. (1860); *Gutenberg*, 1855.
24. Thoischen, E.—Christiansand, Denmark; *Copernicus*, 1852.
25. Thorngrel, J.—Copenhagen, Denmark; *Leibniz*, 1850.
26. Traudgen, Carl 33—Svendborg, Denmark; *Gutenberg*, 1855.
27. Vock, Georg—Benz, Denmark; *Copernicus*, 1852.
28. Weide, Fr. Wilhelm—Flensburg, Denmark; *Copernicus*, 1852.

From *New Homes in a New Land, German Immigration to Texas, 1847-1861* by Ethel Hander Geue.

England, then Quebec. By the time they arrived in America, they had $5 each. It was winter, but they were Danes who knew what cold weather was all about. Unable to find work immediately, they somehow traveled west, following other Danes to the north central states. In Michigan, a Swedish farmer gave them the not too cheerful job of grubbing stumps out of his snow-covered fields.

By spring, the young men had found better work in a sawmill, which gave them enough money to travel south and take a ship for Panama. They were still bound for California. After crossing the isthmus, they embarked on an unlucky ship. Cholera broke out soon after departure.

Christian Andersen and Harry Johnsen watch a burial while taking refuge in the rigging during a cholera epidemic at sea

The Danes climbed high into the rigging with what supplies they could carry and refused to come down. Either their resistance or their altitude was high enough—they did not catch cholera. They survived, grimly watching below as the bodies of other passengers were dropped into the sea.

After three weeks of quarantine at San Francisco, the men did not even want to debark over the gangplank. They jumped into the bay and swam ashore well away from the docks.

Once ashore, the only California gold Andersen and Johnsen saw was their pay from a sawmill where they worked. After a time, the young men wandered back east, overland through Wyoming, Nebraska, then into Kansas at the Oklahoma line where they tried farming. They made two mistakes. They had actually settled on Indian land and were told to move by the Indian agent. They did not take much convincing because the second mistake was that their farm lay right in the path of the Texas cattle drives.

They moved south through Dallas, then on to San Antonio in the spring of 1872, hoping to join a wagon train headed back out west. While at a market area, they met Judge Booker Davenport who invited them to take a look at Bandera and the Texas hill country.

They agreed, but the trip was a slow one. The wagon broke a wheel and one of the team of horses broke a leg. The spring weather and the beautiful country did the rest. The Danes decided they had had enough traveling.

Although Johnsen later did move to Del Rio, Christian looked at and later bought a ranch up Red River Creek. He stayed the rest of his life. Christian became a citizen, married Adeline Klemme of Boerne in 1874, and raised a family of four.

Christian Andersen lived until 1926. His family said that he never really gave up his dream of having a home overlooking San Francisco, paid for with California gold. But a daughter, Lana Anderson Wallace, left a thought that may have been as good: "My father gathered very little California gold to leave to posterity, but he did leave a good name and very sweet memories, and I am glad he was my Dad."

The Gillespie County area attracted a number of Danish families over the years who were often related by marriage, were friends or had heard of central Texas through former acquaintances in Denmark.

One early arrival was Rasmus Frandsen who had gone to America, drifted around for awhile and decided on the central Texas hill country as home. He often wrote back to a former schoolmate, Johan Striegler, telling him how good America was.

Thus Johan Frederick Gottlieb Striegler and his wife Jensine Lange decided to make the journey to Texas. Theirs was no easy decision. Jensine was the daughter of a well-known architect and well-established Danish family. Johan was an educated man, part Norwegian, a talented musician, and owner of a small linen textile mill and a dry goods store. Johan was also the inventor of a loom which promised to have great application in making woolen materials. For a time he was even the owner of two farms in Denmark and was assistant mayor of Svendborg.

But, with a growing family, business was simply not good enough to give the Strieglers the security they wanted. Nor did the opportunities look good enough for their children. And perhaps Johan and his wife liked adventure.

Leaving their businesses and lands in the care of relatives, the family left their homeland. The father Johan was 42 when he made the move with his wife and nine children. In October of 1855, the party of 15 landed at Indianola, Texas, after a seven-week trip. With the family were two servants and two young men who had previously worked in the linen factory. Not incidentally, one of these young men, William Otte, was the fiancee of Antoinette Striegler, the eldest daughter. Agreeing with Antoinette that the Atlantic Ocean would not separate them, he stowed away on the ship. When well out at sea, he revealed his presence and was, perhaps necessarily, welcomed by the family. The couple was later wed in the spring of 1856 at Fredericksburg.

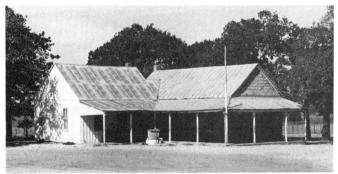

The Rocky Hill School near Fredericksburg

Jensine Lange Striegler

Fredericksburg, c. 1890

O. W. Striegler
and daughter Constance

Arthur and Maria Striegler with children George, Signe and Richmond

The Peter Anderson family who came to Hutto in 1891

Mr. and Mrs. Christian Mathisen

Christian Mathisen at about age 26

Johan Frederick Gottlieb Striegler

Gathering for the golden wedding anniversary of Mr. and Mrs. Ove Striegler, July 1919

After a rough journey by ox cart, the family arrived at the Rasmus Frandsen home where they were to stay until they could build their own house. Johan bought a parcel of land near the Rocky Hill community, where other Danish families were later to settle and finished a house there.

While the men set about getting a farm going, building houses and animal shelters, making furniture and farm equipment; the women set up housekeeping. They took care of the younger children, cooked, sewed, made soap and candles, knitted stockings and scarves, and prepared any farm surplus for market in town. What food could be raised was supplemented by deer, fish, squirrel, wild turkey and ducks, honey, wild grapes, plums and pecans—all abundant in the Pedernales River valley.

Around 1860, Johan and his three oldest sons became United States citizens— just in time for secession and the Civil War. The three older sons joined the Confederate army; and the two youngest, and their father, served in the Home Guard and trucked freight to Mexico during the years of the Federal blockade.

Johan died in November of 1872 and was, according to the family, well satisfied with his move to a new land.

One of his sons, Frederick Christian, remained on the family farm for awhile, then at 21, after the Civil War, joined the Texas Rangers. He served until 1871 in the San Saba area, then worked as a cowboy on the Chisholm trail, returning to Texas with wagons of trade goods. Frederick evidently tired of wandering, for he returned to central Texas and married Mary Louise Mogford. The couple reared a large family and lived the rest of their lives in central Texas.

Another son, Arthur, started his adult life as a mail carrier, then entered Civil War service as an interpreter. He could speak English, French, German and Spanish in addition to his native Danish. After some post-war years as a cattleman, Arthur managed the family farm until 1887. Going back to Denmark for a visit, Arthur there met Marie Lorentzen. Denmark, particularly in the company of Marie, was attractive, but he decided not to stay. Back in Texas, he became a public surveyor in 1891 when he was 51 and worked for several counties. In the meantime, Marie had become his fiancee. She arrived in Galveston in 1892, where they were married.

Arthur gave the land at Rocky Hill for the local school which became the community school for children of the area. Establishing their home nearby, they raised their three children on a farm for a number of years, then moved into Fredericksburg after the turn of the century.

The Striegler family, including many other individuals, became a well-known family, contributing outstanding citizens to Texas, California and England.

And the Danes, a few, spread out over Texas in these years. Most of them found prosperity enough for a family and pleasant times; some bear stories of success and some of trouble.

In 1891, the Andersen family arrived in central Texas from Denmark via Galveston. This family left again, returning to Denmark in 1904 because of the promise of receiving land there. The promise was not fulfilled and the family found itself financially unable to return to America. Perhaps as a compromise, the daughters, Katrine Anine and Jensine Andrea, returned alone to make new lives for themselves.

John Sorenson came to Texas in 1872 and worked as a bricklayer near Dallas. In the late 1870's, Sorenson worked on the Galveston, Harrisburg and San Antonio Railroad, but later moved to New Mexico where he became a contractor. He started doing military contract work and moved on to El Paso in 1880 to work on buildings at Ft. Bliss. Sorenson remained in town, starting his own brick yard and contracting for most of the first brick buildings in town.

Frederick D. Bader came to Texas as a member of the Commissary Department of the United States army in 1866. Bader served for a time in the State Police, then later as a Bexar County deputy sheriff.

A few Danes made Williamson County their home. Some families moved into the Frame Switch and Hutto areas, largely from other areas of Texas. The first blacksmith in Hutto was Carl "Cap" Hansen, a Dane who helped immigrant families set up homes in the area during the 1880's.

Thus, the Danes came in small numbers, had many vocations and were found in most areas of the state. The story of Christian Mathisen shows the effect of a good recommendation by a countryman. This was a common way for Danes to learn of a new, possibly better, homeland.

Before 1890, Søren Hoisager and others like Jens Hansen had settled in the Stonewall area. Jens, a sea captain from the island of Sejerø, traded his heavy overcoat for a cow and his gold watch for a horse to set himself up as a central Texas farmer. Søren decided to return to Denmark to visit his family. There, he met Christian Mathisen. Christian had just finished his apprenticeship as a blacksmith and was about to start traveling, hoping to build up trade for himself and even perhaps find a permanent location.

Meeting Hoisager and hearing his description of the Texas hill country, however, changed things. Mathisen, and Hoisager's sister, decided to go to America with Søren. According to family tradition, Christian's motive was curiosity. By November of 1890, the three were in Texas. Christian spent that Christmas at the farm of Jens Hansen, in the company of fellow Danes, but far from home.

Within one year, Hoisager's stories were proven correct. The new land was a good place to live—good for a new home. Christian's father, Mathis

Mathisen, his mother and their other children—Christine, Marius, Julia, Annie, Walter, and Andrea—joined the move from Stenderup, Denmark, to the Fredericksburg area.

Christian and his father set up a blacksmithing business, including Mathis's occupations as wheelwright and cabinetmaker. They repaired all sorts of machinery, shod horses, and made plows and wagons. What may have been the first gasoline engine in the county was used to power the lathe and even run an elevator in the building. Their shop operated in a small building on Main Street in Fredericksburg. Christian Kraus, a German settler, built the structure, and it served first as the Mathisen's place of business, then as the home of Christian and Emily Striegler after their marriage. Christian's father lived next door, and there were other Danish families in the area.

In the neighborhood, the Mathisens maintained a number of Danish customs including the traditional Christmas Eve dinner, a gathering of families for each birthday and occasional songs in Danish.

No effort was made to teach Danish, so only that which was spoken in Mathis's and Christian's generation prevailed. In fact, in this area of predominant German settlement, Christian's children learned German during their first school years along with English. There was no apparent Danish-German rivalry in the Texas hill country—unlike common conditions in Europe. In fact, many of the Danish families intermarried quickly with the Germans who had preceded them by nine or so years.

Christian Mathisen and his wife Emily Striegler are remembered for their story telling. Emily had a great store of fairy tales, not the least of which were the same as those written by Hans Christian Andersen. Christian, by contrast, had tales of the pagan gods, Odin and Thor, and he told the stories in verse—with great conviction. He always had an appropriate story to illustrate any happening of the day. But Danish was not spoken in the home, and only one rhyme—a Danish children's poem fancifully naming the fingers of the hand—survives in the family: *"Tommeltot, Slikkepot, Langemand, Guldibrand, Lille Peter Spillemand."*

Christian was always an active man and a person highly thought of by his neighbors. In addition to his founding work with the Fredericksburg National Farm Loan Association, he had more unusual activities. Near the turn of the century, long before there was a question of energy supply, Christian built a wind-powered electric generator. In those early years, however, there was no practical use for the strange device and the children would play with it, drawing mild but quite respectable shocks from the apparatus.

Christian, however, was particularly known for working with the farm loan program and other activities such as rural free mail delivery, local telephone systems and innovative agricultural methods.

The entire family was an active one. Marius, Christian's brother, produced a tubeless automobile tire in San Antonio in World War I years, but it was a device ahead of its time. His compact radio antenna was more practical.

Today, one of Christian's daughters, Colonel Louise Mathisen Ergas, is retired after a lifetime of military nursing. She, a former operating room chief and chief anaesthetist at Fort Sam Houston Base Hospital, served in World War II. After the war she served in Hawaii, Germany and occupied Japan. Fred Mathisen is a leading Fredericksburg businessman and rancher engaged in a host of civic activities, and Mrs. Myrtle Maren Mathisen Westerfeldt is now a retired teacher having experience from college physics down to the first grade.

And today, these descendants, and scores of others from the Danish families, live in the area. As far as some Danish Texans are concerned, the hill country is home.

Hans Gammel, who was to become a well-known Danish Texan indeed, arrived in 1877. He was later *the* bookman of Texas: collector, seller, publisher, and undisputed bibliophile of Texana and western titles. He already had quite a bit of activity behind him when he came to Texas.

Karl Hans Peter Marius Nielsen Gamel, who was to become H. P. N. Gammel in America, was born in 1854 in Grenaa, Jylland. His father, Niels Hansen, and mother, Mette Marie Jensen Brugger, had eight children, four of whom died young. Hans, however, was a robust young man, hard working and, in his words, "always in trouble."

What Hans's father did is not known now. He was either a small land holder near town or a miller. Hans worked as a farm laborer when young, bringing in extra money to the family. Times were fairly hard, and Hans's brother Niels and two sisters, Minnie and Sena, left for America.

Hans worked hard. "I grew up at 15 and was a full grown man at 16." He was strongly built, active all his life, and wore rather long blond hair. Hans, like many a young man, did not like schoolrooms, but he did like to read, an interest that would shape his later life.

At 16, Hans fell in love. "He . . . saw Marie and wanted to get married. I had to lay my case before the King who authorized the marriage before I was of age. I got my papers, married, worked hard. And after a year or more we had a sweet baby born to us."

Hans married Anna Marie Andersen, soon had a family, and equally soon, found himself in the common condition of so many other Danes. Life could be lived, but not nearly so well as one wished.

In 1874, Hans's sister Minnie came home from America for a visit. When she returned, Hans went with her "to dig some gold and send for the family."

Arriving in New York, Hans traveled to Chicago where he stayed with his other sister, Sena. There, his brother Niels came by and they teamed up to make their way in the new land.

Both Hans and Niels had what the family called "jolly" disposition. In fact, they were hardworking optimists. The brothers soon had jobs as traveling salesmen, dressed up in fine suits, selling inexpensive jewelry. Niels had learned the ways of America, and so did Hans, who did not like to be taken for a greenhorn. Hans had some trouble at first with language. He learned to say "ham and eggs" and ordered only this breakfast until his English improved. That took awhile. In later years, he did not care so much for the dish.

But he kept traveling and selling cheap jewelry until he knew English and much of America. The brothers traveled to the young towns of the west and the older ones of the east. They saw other immigrants—much like themselves—populating the great plains and crossing the Rockies. They traveled with settlers and desperadoes, families and rootless men.

"What we did and how," Hans later said, "is a dead letter. I never killed anybody and never robbed anybody and I hardly ever carried a gun except (when) deputized. I will say I was with many desperate men, knew them but never was in trouble with them. I would drink but never got drunk. If I did drink, I would never fight."

It was a good enough set of rules for living in the early American west. Hans survived and soon had brought his wife and daughter to Chicago. Then he and Niels went south. They arrived in Galveston in 1877, stayed in Houston for awhile, and were in Austin the next year. Hans liked the small capital city and wrote his wife that it was a good place, but told her she could not join him just then because he had lost most of his money through a bit of gambling in Houston. Young Marie wrote back that money or no money, she was coming down. That decided Hans's permanent home. Marie and their daughter were soon in town, and Hans worked at a host of activities to keep the family together and food on the table.

Hans rented a place on Congress Avenue and set up shop as a merchant, selling whatever he could: writing paper for soldiers and freighters, jewelry and lemonade. He worked with two other Danes supplying poles for telegraph lines and worked at other odd jobs around town. Behind the store he set up a combination bedroom, parlor and dining room.

"We lived high," Hans wrote later, "with a bed made of some old boxes and a table and 2 chairs I bought for 40¢."

One day Hans bought 24 books for 25¢. First he read them to improve his English, then he put them out on a shelf in a chinaberry tree in front of his shop. They sold. Gammel found out that Texans like himself did read, and he soon

The Colonial Capitol, Austin, c. 1880

Congress Avenue, Austin, c. 1875

Hans Peter Nielsen Gammel

*Site of the Gammel-Statesman Publishing
Company on Congress Avenue, Austin*

*The Colonial Capitol in Austin after
the fire of November 1881*

was regularly buying books for 5¢ and selling them for a dime. This was the start of one of the most famous bookstores and private collections of books in the state.

Gammel moved to several locations in Austin, once even to El Paso for a short time, but did not ever swerve from his interest in books. His business at first was a ten-cent store, where he sold all sorts of items, but the books gradually took over. Austinites called his store "a bookstand where lemonade was sold on Saturdays" or "a lemonade stand with books and trinkets for sale also." It was soon to be nationally known.

Gammel's window displays became legendary. Once, he bought a cheap violin and put it in his front window—with a price tag of $2500.00. He made up a wonderful story about a Dane who, at the end of an incredibly difficult journey, played the instrument for the king. The violin did attract browsers. Much later, a stranger stopped by when the store was filled with regular customers and to their amusement asked to buy the violin for $2.50. He had apparently misread the marked price. "Sold," Gammel said and hastily concluded the deal to everyone's amazement. The violin had already done its job, of course, and H. P. N. Gammel went on to other unusual window displays.

Gammel's life in Austin was a varied one, complete with its share of sadness. Late in 1880, his wife died of typhoid, and he and his daughter were hospitalized for weeks. Finally recovered, Gammel found himself almost alone. Even his brother was in some unknown place. "When I got up, my little business was gone, wife gone, brother gone. Baby was all I had."

But Gammel was not down for long. He was then 27, and he started again. About a year later, Gammel attended a camp meeting north of Austin. At these religious revivals, ministers often resorted to various offers to keep interest high. The minister in charge of the weeks-long camp offered to perform the first marriage ceremony absolutely free during the course of the meetings.

On the first day, Gammel met a young Swedish woman, Josephine Matilda Ledel. She had been sent to Texas to live with relatives when her family had drifted into difficult financial straits. Now 16, she planned to return to Sweden but, within a few days, found herself very much in love with Gammel. They took up the minister's offer. Hans wrote of his marriage as "an incident of interest . . . that was entirely out of the book business." But he always understated his enthusiasms—it was a match that was to last the rest of their lives.

A few months later, an event took place that was to have a singular effect on Gammel's life. About noon on Wednesday, November 9, 1881, the state capitol building caught fire, probably from a defective stove. In a matter of hours, it was gutted on the cool, rainy day. State officials saved what they could, but the local water pressure was too low to fight the fire, and soon the building was a collapsed, smoldering ruin, gradually watersoaked in a slow, winter rain.

Inside had been the records of the state for 36 years, the Republic of Texas, and even documents dating to Mexican and Spanish times: land titles, laws, census figures, transcribed speeches, letters and tax records. And in these things, Gammel had a great interest. He secured salvage rights to the building and a small salary in return for removing the rubble.

Before the winter weather could add to the damage, the husky Dane waded into the mass of charred furniture, papers, walls and cabinets, dressed in hip boots and overalls. He would often work all day, his wife bringing his lunch to the ruins. Hans removed the rubble, but the papers of state went back to his house. There, he and Josephine hung the documents on clotheslines to dry, inside the house and out. They cleaned what they could and ironed wrinkled papers. Josephine was not too happy about the job at first. She agreed with the neighbors—it was quite a sight—but Hans's enthusiasm about the salvaged documents was infectuous. It became a challenge: the papers should not be lost and later there might be a use for them. The documents were stored with the family belongings of the newlyweds. They lay idle for a long time. Long enough for Hans to enter the publishing business.

This activity started in 1890 with *Early Times in Texas* and included many other titles, but the largest venture was the *Laws of Texas, 1822-1897.* This initial ten-volume work, later expanded to thirty, was an instant and overwhelming success. The volumes depended heavily on the salvaged state papers which C. W. Raines, the state librarian, helped Gammel put into shape. The set was an instant classic and remains so to this day: the fundamental collection of Texas law.

Hans Gammel salvages papers from the remains of the capitol fire of 1881

46

Gammel's success was assured, even though stormy days as a state printer and unsuccessful ventures into Texas oil and New Mexico meerschaum were also his lot.

Gammel did some land buying and selling over much of Texas, including parcels in Rains, Ward, Loving and Liberty Counties and town lots in Lubbock, Galveston and Harlingen, but with no great profit. He even bought chances in the Danish Colonial Class lottery, but his store continued to be the chief source of income and, other than the *Laws of Texas*, the occupation for which he was most well known.

Gammel's varying letterheads became collectors' items. One printed in 1917 read "The Oldest Book Store in the State, Established in 1877. The proprietor, Gammel, was born in Denmark, rich and good looking—not so now." Another listed his business references as "Mrs. H. P. N. Gammel, her three boys and five girls, and a few other friends." He also printed a "Public Notice" that said "... H. P. N. Gammel is guaranteed safe and solid by his long time friend, H. P. N. Gammel."

One letterhead gave his company rundown: "Capital Stocks $000,000.00; Director: H. P. N. Gammel; President: H. P. N. Gammel; Vice-President: H. P. N. Gammel; and Secretary-Treasurer: H. P. N. Gammel." His invoices bore the famous "If it's a book . . . Get it at Gammel's."

And at his desk, book orders and shipment notes were kept on fragments of paper sacks, envelopes, tablet pages, the backs of wedding invitations and post cards.

Hans's personal collection of books relating to Texas became famous. He always maintained he was no expert but was certainly considered so in all matters of books. In addition, his store had the largest holdings of literature, law and Texana titles in the state.

Gammel was always a friendly and predictable presence in his store. He wore fine suits but apparently always had on the same black string tie—he kept 24 of them, exactly alike in wear. His business desk was complete with a trained mouse, and his dog Bill had a charge account at the nearby market and drug store. At home, Gammel entertained with his famous Copenhagen punch, the composition of which remained a secret even from friends—it was in fact the remains of the bottles in his liquor cabinet, whatever that might be at the time of compounding. But Gammel was no eccentric. To him, these "jollities" were as real as his book collection and his family—no less a part of his life.

Gammel died in February of 1931, a year after Josephine, leaving married daughters and sons to carry on the business for a time. It perhaps was not the same, for Gammel was a part of the bookstore and his personal collections. The latter passed into the Vandale collection, then to The University of Texas.

And today, the initials G.P.L. have a special meaning to Texana book collectors. When Gammel would acquire a particularly rare item, it would go into his private library, where people were free to read, but seldom to borrow. Gammel's sons would say to later dealers that a title was in "papa's private library." This was gradually converted to "Granpa's Private Library" which referred to a rare and wonderful book indeed. Today, the "G.P.L. item" can also be counted on to drain the pocketbook.

VI.
Danevang:
The Danish Field

The first group of Danes who could be called a colony came to Texas in 1894. Land on the coastal plain had been bought by the Dansk Folkesamfund, the Danish People's Society. In southwest Wharton County, the society hoped to found a colony where Danish culture and language might be preserved.

A branch of the Danish Lutheran Church also supported the effort as a Church colony. This interest had started some years earlier and arose in part from a Church dispute in Denmark. Around 1870 (officially from 1894) the Evangelical Danish Lutherans in America split into two synods. The break created the Danish Evangelical Lutheran Church and the United Danish Lutheran Church, close in name, but indicating a rift perhaps greater between Danish Americans than between Danes in Denmark.

The Danish Evangelical Lutheran Church, the branch or synod to have the Texas colony as its religious charge, was composed of the followers of N.F.S. Grundtvig—clergyman, philosopher, poet, historian and prophet of the mild, low-church side of Danish Lutheranism. Adherents were known as the "happy Danes." The United Church members were known as the "holy Danes," "gloomy Danes," or the Home or Inner Mission people—a much sterner group. The Danes did not adhere as strongly to a national church as the Norwegian and Swedish immigrants, but the Lutheran split did affect them. At times, the two branches of the church worked against each other, founding rival colonies and settlement areas, and actually contributing to a faster assimilation of Danes into American life. The United Church, much more pro-assimilation, was also much more successful in increasing membership.

The Texas colony—Danevang—started with the desire of the Danish Lutheran Church for a colony and the wish of the Dansk Folkesamfund, the sponsoring society, for a place to preserve Danish culture.

The bulk of the society's members were in the north central United States, where most of the Danes had first settled: Illinois, Wisconsin, Minnesota, Iowa, North and South Dakota, Nebraska and Kansas. F. L. Grundtvig, youngest son of the Danish clergyman, had come to Wisconsin on his honeymoon and dreamed of coastal colonies to the south. These were to be founded in the name of the society and in behalf of the church movement his father had represented. In fact, he and other friends had founded the Dansk Folkesamfund in 1887 to start further colonial efforts in America. Soon, an Iowan, J. C. Evers, was appointed by the folk society to look at Texas land as part of a three-man land committee, the Landudvalg.

Before the turn of the 19th century, most of Wharton County, Texas, was ranch country, much of it owned by the Texas Land and Cattle Company. Evers, after looking at various areas in the south, was shown this land, a grassy plain covered with thousands of cattle. It was indeed a tempting sight. Discarding earlier possibilities, the committee took an option with the company for the sale of 25,000 acres to people of Danish extraction.

The price was to be $9.00 an acre, paid for by the settlers at a rate of $1.00 per acre cash down payment, with only the interest on the remaining $8.00 per acre in the second year. Thereafter, they were to pay $1.00 per acre per year, plus the interest. Now this, even then, was a good deal. A land holder near Chicago could sell off his holdings and buy many times more land in Texas for the same money. The young family who could not find a place to their liking in the Dakotas might get a little cash together for a small parcel of Texas land, and there was an added advantage in living with a group of countrymen.

Whatever the desires of the Dansk Folkesamfund, the settlers were looking for cheap land and a place to raise a family. In fact, the Danish settlers did not become land barons. Only two of the original 78 families bought the maximum of 320 acres.

Evers's contract called for the sale of 8000 acres of land the first year. If this was done, the land company would give 160 acres for a school and church site. The Dansk Folkesamfund was to receive 25¢ per acre from the transaction, a part of which paid Evers's salary.

Although some Danes were to come directly from Denmark to the new colony, later in 1905, Evers did his main recruiting in the north central states.

In August of 1894, the first colonists arrived. According to most records, Jens Peter Olson was the first to buy land on August 17, 1894. Olson, from Holbaek, Sjaelland, was followed by over 70 initial families whose names included

Mogensen, Larsen, Rasmussen, Madsen, Hansen, Krag, Thomsen, Lykke, Andersen, Nygaard, Hermansen, Treumer, Christensen, Wind, Ravn, Berndt, Petersen and Jorgensen. Not all stayed. One man, Mogensen, built a home but returned rather quickly to Chicago. His house was thereafter used as shelter by some of the settlers the first year.

An arrival at Danevang, 1894

What the first settlers saw when they arrived was a flat, grass-covered plain as far as the eye could see with trees here and there only along the low streams. No wonder they named it Danevang, the Danish field. Tres Palacios Creek lay about four miles to the east, and Juanita and Willow Creeks to the west. El Campo, the closest settlement, was about ten miles north over a dirt trail that was soon a dirt road. The area north had been settled earlier by Spanish and Mexican families, later Anglos, Swedes, Norwegians, Czechs and Germans. Danevang was known in the north United States as "the Danish Colony, El Campo, Texas," for a time.

J. P. Olson came somewhat before his wife and family. He had, incidentally, changed the spelling of his name from Olsen because "Olson" was more American—to his eye. He arrived, picked out and bought his land, then returned for his family.

The Olsons came from Kansas in January of 1895, riding in a rented railroad freight car with their daughter, family belongings, furniture and livestock. When the family got to Rosenberg, on their way west to El Campo, they were not allowed to ride in such manner on the Southern Pacific line. They had to move to a passenger car. Finally arriving, they stayed at the hotel in El Campo while their house was finished.

By February, many of the first colonists had arrived, but it was to a bleak scene. From an unknown cause, the lush prairie grass had burned, leaving a plain of black ash. Sine Nygaard recalled that, after being welcomed by the burned, silent prairie, the next day rain fell, turning the ash into a sea of black mud. This was followed by snow. Some of the cattle the Danes brought died from starvation.

The Danes had come to Texas with a background of north-country farming experience. They knew how to raise cold-weather grains and livestock. With a trace of overconfidence, some thought of showing the Texans how farming should be done. The northern crops they tried would not grow, and unfamiliar cattle diseases killed the livestock they had shipped in.

The farmers with families to support had even more problems. Of the pioneer life, some said simply, "It was toil and drudgery." But they also said that the Danes were ones to hold their ground.

Their first homes were primitive and the flat plain, flooded so much that ploughing was at times impossible, was more than disappointing. It was a disaster. The first year the Danes lived mainly on chickens, deer, berries and sweet potatoes.

F. L. Grundtvig and Evers visited the colony in 1895. Grundtvig held church services in Mads Andersen's home. That summer, Ingeborg Olson was born, the first child born in Danevang and was baptized by Grundtvig. Mrs. Mads Andersen died in the same year, the first to be buried in the cemetery.

Andrea Nielsen was a young Danish woman, married for five years to Marcus, a farmer and blacksmith, when they decided to move from the midwest to Danevang. They had heard of the colony through Evers, who was always recruiting people and traveling with them to Texas.

Marcus bought 160 acres of the colony's land, between two creeks. This proved to be a mistake, for after rains, the land would stand in water for several days. Marcus eventually had to build small levees to keep back the water. He ploughed with oxen at first because the horses they brought died in a general plague. Marcus soon found out that cotton was the best money crop.

When Andrea arrived, she remembered the drive from El Campo as long miles of mud. After a rain the nine miles seemed like 900. The wagon wheels repeatedly fouled and had to be cleaned. When she arrived, Mrs. Christian Rasmussen had bread, pastry and coffee ready to welcome her but also broke into tears, saying, "I'm so unhappy here."

Andrea found her first home in the south full of bedbugs. She and her husband put the bedposts in pans of water thinking this would keep the vermin from crawling up and into bed, but the bugs then dropped on the sleeping couple from the ceiling.

"I'll have to admit," Andrea said, "that I cried nearly every evening." And Evers and Grundtvig, going back to Iowa after their visit in 1895, sat on the train and also cried. Even their hopes for the colony were low.

The initial payments on the land could not be met. Herman Kuntz, president of the Texas Land and Cattle Company, visited Danevang, however, and was so impressed with the determination of the Danes that there was no difficulty getting an extension on the bank notes. In fact, when asked by an outsider why he did not foreclose, a representative of the banking firm said he would not "kill the goose which in time would lay golden eggs."

The Danes observed farming conditions in Texas and learned to raise southern crops. Turning mainly to cotton, they soon had crops that gave the little community its first economic base. In fact, H. P. Hermansen wrote an article for more northern Danish readers, giving a description of the strange plant called cotton. The men raised pigs, then smoked bacon by the traditional Danish method in a barrel, and sold these with surplus dairy products processed by the women. They knew how to solve their problems. Against hardship, the earlier settlers said "we kept our ears stiff" and gradually made headway. The first carpenter in the colony was C. A. Nygaard who stayed for the first six years during the first major building period. He then moved on to Galveston.

Margrethe Henningsen remembered the rather uncooperative cows—even the "Danish" ones. Her family had gotten a cow from Iver Wind and they had high hopes.

"Mother stood with pail in her hand for now we were really going to have milk, cream and butter; but, alas, when Mother sat down to milk, both she and the pail landed in the grass. Father and Mr. Wind tied the cow . . . then Mother tried again. But the monster jumped into the air with all four legs."

This cow was exchanged for another, but the new one was a Texan. "We looked askance at the new cow, for it was a real Texas cow with long horns out to the sides. But it proved to be quite gentle as long as there was enough cotton seed in the feedbag. It was just a matter of getting through first. If the cow finished eating first, she ran, and then we either had to get more feed or content ourselves with what milk we had."

But the climate proved to be worse than the strange cows. The Colorado River, some ten miles east, would flood the whole country, so much that one could go by boat almost anywhere. Before the days of upriver dams and flood control, residents saw the Brazos and Colorado Rivers join into one sheet of water scores of miles wide. Most homes were built up on blocks, about a foot above the ground, both to escape the water and to be cooler in the summer. Even so, after high water, mud would have to be shoveled off the first floor. And a trip to the outhouse was sometimes only possible in high boots, sometimes not possible at all.

By the end of 1895, ninety-three families had purchased over 9,000 acres, and more settlers were coming. Many of the Danes had come originally from Schleswig or the islands of Fyn and Sjaelland, but most parts of Denmark were represented. Since there was some dialect difference, the standard "national" Danish language was used. Most of the Danes had lived in Illinois, Iowa, Wisconsin, Minnesota, Nebraska, Kansas or the Dakotas for a little while and were used to some language changes.

The colony even attracted Danes from other places in Texas. Andreas and Karen Marie Zarine Fredericksen came from Vejle, Jylland, to San Antonio in 1890 but moved to Danevang in 1896.

The goal of the first 8,000 acres was reached, but the entire total of 25,000 acres set aside was never bought by the settlers. Some was sold to others by the holding company. By 1898, about 13,000 acres were sold to 150 Danish buyers. The Dansk Folkesamfund i Amerika had received the extra land for selling the first quota and in turn sold 40 acres to the church for $1.00—the only restriction being that if the congregation ever seceded from the Danish Evangelical Lutheran Church, they would forfeit the land. Twenty acres on Tres Palacios Creek was given to the church as a park and picnic area for the members of the colony.

Peter N. Thomsen and his wife came to Danevang after seven years of indifferent fortune in Illinois. He had improved his lot from 29 acres, a small house, one table, six chairs, a bedstead and one wash pot to four horses, a cow and calf, farming equipment and a fair collection of furniture.

Deciding on the move to Danevang, Thomsen loaded his animals and belongings into a railroad boxcar for the journey south to Houston. Thomsen was milking the cow as the train arrived in town. It was Christmas. Then, as now, milking had to be done every day, Christmas or travel or anything—there are no vacations. Suddenly, the train was derailed by accident, and the boxcar smashed down the roadbed, throwing the cow upside down into one end of the car and Thomsen, equally upside down, among the farm tools. Not seriously injured, he crawled from the wreck and angrily reproached the train crew. He only received their comment that "It is Christmas day, and one couldn't expect anything else."

It took him a little longer to get to El Campo, then Danevang, than he had expected.

The Danes built a community meeting hall in 1895 and established their post office the same year along with their own school and U.S. Weather Station. H. P. Hermansen was both postmaster and weather observer. After initial meetings in Mads Andersen's home, the church services were held in the meeting hall by the Reverend L. Henningsen, and the meetings were a great comfort to the settlers.

Reverend S. H. Madsen.
Danevang pastor when
the first church
was finished, 1909

Jens Peter Olsen
of Danevang

The church at Danevang, 1911

Community house at Danevang, c. 1896

The "East" Danevang school

Gathering at the Danevang Community Hall

Pastor Johannes Ravn and family, 1913

Mr. and Mrs. H. P. Jensen,
Danevang

Ella Hansen and Emma
Petersen at Danevang

L. J. Lykke farm, Danevang

P. J. Agerskov Petersen farm at Danevang, 1906

The Petersen farm, Danevang

The Hansen brothers plowing a field at Danevang

Christian Madsen and his wife Kristen on their
farm at Danevang, c. 1900

Danevang school and students in 1908

Group at the church picnic grounds at Trespalacios Creek near Danevang

P. J. Agerskov Petersen and wife
Johanna with their children

The Danes felt a great sense of community and were quick to help one another. In fact, at church baptisms, not only the godparents, but the entire congregation would also rise to indicate their total support for the new community member.

The Danevang settlers were and are known for their community singing. Almost any public gathering, party, and certainly church service was filled with song. The first pastor, Rev. Henningsen, remarked "That the people are fully alive is immediately evident by their exceptionally hearty singing." And even in the worst times, the Danes never seemed to be without their magnificently brewed, cheerful coffee and pastry, the ingredients for which were brought from El Campo—a trip which could take from before sunrise to after sunset.

The first ministers were native Danes and needed a multitude of talents themselves to survive in this new frontier on an average of $15 a month. The Reverend S. H. Madsen, for example, served also as a doctor, making use of his own carbolic ointment. He repaired watches and sewing machines. Most ministers raised what food they could in a garden next to the meeting hall. Such versatility was considered admirable—but it was also necessary. The first minister, Rev. Henningsen, had a salary of $101.15 in 1896; and Madsen's annual salary was $300 from the colony and $100 from the Danish Folk Society.

And Texas was itself a strange place. When the Henningsens arrived, they were delighted with the "lark and the roses of the prairie" but not so much taken with the nearby ranch cattle that would wander over and scratch themselves on the first, rather shaky houses. The land around the settlers was still open range land, owned and stocked by a large cattle company. Mrs. Ella Hansen remembers when as a young child she was once grabbed by her mother and carried into the house just ahead of a stampede of cows across the yard.

Like everyone else, the Henningsens did not like the absence of trees around the houses—soon planted—nor the mud. This family remembered the early day picnics over at Tres Palacios Creek under oaks draped with Spanish moss. They considered the strange Spanish moss a "holiday dress" for the trees. Fishing would fill the afternoon, with the men netting in the creek and the women making an evening meal of fried fish. Along the treelined creeks were wild grapes and dewberries which were gathered in season as a special treat.

Occasionally, community members would decide on a tree planting day. The men of the settlement would donate a day to transplanting native trees to locations around the community hall or church. They usually selected quick growing trees from the nearby streams: cottonwoods, chinaberries, mulberries and sycamores.

P. J. Agerskov Petersen was a slightly later arrival in the colony who became the local historian both of the church and the settlement, as well as a successful farmer.

Petersen, who soon added the name of his hometown, Agerskov, to his name because he felt there were too many Petersens around, heard of the colony and bought 40 acres on a visit. But the young man did not have the immediate means to start farming, so he went to Galveston to work on the wharves.

Not only did he make enough money to sponsor his farming, but he found a wife, Johanne Hansen from Fyn. She had departed Denmark for Michigan, but after folk high school training, left for Galveston to start a Scandinavian Seaman's Mission Home. Although this was later a financial failure, she met Petersen and married him in Galveston. The couple lived there a few years, then moved to Danevang.

Johanne Petersen arrived in February of 1900 after a cold journey from Galveston with her four-week-old daughter. "When I reached El Campo, my husband was at the station with the buggy and a pair of fast horses. We were soon in the seat, warmly tucked in with shawls and blankets, and we hardly felt the penetrating cold. After a while we came to our little home. Our good friend, Ivar Wind, was nailing a flag to the gable of the house. We quickly entered the warm room. The coffee was steaming, and a huge bowl of *aebleskiver* (a Danish popover dusted with sugar) awaited us on the table. From the music box came the song 'Two thrush sat upon the beech twig.' It was a festive reception. When spring came the cotton was planted, and we made a little vegetable garden and two large flower gardens."

Their farm was soon one of the most well-ordered and Johanne's flower gardens were always most colorful. Their home was a stopping place for travelers and at times a visiting place for new arrivals. The couple was active in community affairs and even directed amateur theatrical presentations in the colony.

Agerskov Petersen was one of the "most Danish" settlers. Danish was spoken in the home and the children remember the ever-present folk tales in the evenings (most of them from Hans Christian Andersen or the Brothers Grimm). It was said that, although Agerskov-Petersen did not reject English "his spiritual thinking was based on the Danish." And indeed more than the spiritual: for years his name, or the initials "P.J.A-P.," was the byline on many an article on Danevang published in American Danish-language newspapers and magazines.

Little by little, new houses were built, crops were raised, children were born and the rather inhospitable plain became a home. The turning point seemed to come after the Galveston storm of 1900. This hurricane devastated Galveston and also Danevang, among other coastal communities. The cotton crop was wiped out. The Danes almost decided to abandon the colony. Even the minister lost hope. He advised the settlers to burn what buildings were left, then he would lead them away, riding in front on his pony and singing hymns. Hymns or no, the settlers did not like the suggestion—or did not have the money to make another move. A few left in search of other jobs but most stayed. From 1900 on, times were better. *Fremskridt* (progress) was the byword and the old timers later called 1901 the "golden year." The depression many of the settlers felt at first was overcome.

Soon, the Danes had started a cooperative economic system. Such efforts were common in Denmark, and it came naturally to the settlers. It started in general in the spirit of cooperation necessary to survive, and in detail with a supply of bug poison bought for the whole community to protect the cotton. But the settlers went on to bigger things. The Danes established a fire insurance company which was organized in 1897 and incorporated in 1901. The first local cotton gin was built in 1897 by Marcus Nielsen. A telephone exchange was started in 1913 and successfully operated until 1948 when the system was sold to Southwestern Bell. Old timers say the modern service is almost as good as the cooperative system they built themselves, and the rates are only fifteen times higher.

The Danevang Farmer's Cooperative Society was organized in 1920 and incorporated the next year. This association coordinated the marketing of local crops and bought supplies needed by the members at better prices than could be had individually. This organization led to the purchasing of feed in 1922, farm equipment in 1923, a cooperative gin in 1927, a gasoline station in 1932 and a cooperative grocery in Danevang in 1939. The latter came to pass after 17 years of careful discussion. The Danes proceeded in a thoroughly democratic but occasionally slow manner.

In fact, the cooperative associations even bought household appliances for the families at wholesale rates, somewhat to the consternation of commercial dealers in nearby towns.

Even the coffin supply was handled cooperatively at first. A carpenter would be hired at a reduced rate to build five of various sizes at one time. These were kept in the community hall until needed.

One of Danevang's purposes was to preserve the Danish way of life and this, besides an economic base and the church, called for education. The first public school was started in 1895 at the community hall, and local efforts were continuous until consolidation with the El Campo schools in 1951.

Until 1941, the church summer school instruction included Biblical history and Danish history, literature and geography. The day closed occasionally with the story hour common to Danish American summer schools. Even some of the songs in summer school told stories of Danish history. The usual "American" subjects were taught during the regular school year. Even these classes were taught, until around 1938, only by people of Danish background. Three one-room schools were built in 1909, and in 1918 a larger school was built which even included high school grades until the late 1940's.

In the early years, Danish was the local language of business, home and church. In the schools, however, Danish was taught only in the summer and English formed the backbone of the instruction because it was evident that, Danish colony or not, English was the language to learn for any sort of future in the United States.

For the older adults, however, there was the Tylvten Club, the "twelve," composed of twelve families. A set of Danish books would be ordered with dues, then circulated among the members. The club disbanded as English became more common.

The church congregation had met first in homes and then mainly in the community hall after being founded on May 24, 1895, and the first ministers had lived in the hall or temporarily with other families. In 1902, a parsonage was built, allowing the ministers a regular home, and by the winter of 1908-9 the Ansgar Evangelical Lutheran Church was built. Its bell could be heard for miles and in the first years was not just sounded on Sunday, but at each sunrise and sunset. In 1908, Danevang had 64 families on the church roster, by 1919, the church membership listed 464 individuals—and noted there were 80 others living there not on the church roles.

The first automobile was in Danevang in 1911, but the highway from El Campo was not paved until 1931. H. P. Jensen carried the U.S. mail over this road every day except Sundays from 1902 to 1914 with a mule and a cart or buggy. And he would do this for an annual stipend of $500. Because of this mail delivery, he soon was known locally as "Uncle Sam."

The coastal plain was subject to severe storms and although tree wind-breaks were planted for some relief, the winds have little to stop them on the flat coast. Andrea Nielsen remembered the storm of 1909 as the worst. Her husband had driven into El Campo on a hot, sultry morning, and by one o'clock in the afternoon, a gusty downpour moved through the little settlement. She was in the house with her six-year-old son, then expecting what was to be her last child, Lillian. "One thing I was thankful for and that was that the Negro, George Peters and his family, came in to spend the night in the storeroom." Her other children were caught at school by the storm and were taken to a nearby cellar to weather out the evening.

The storm grew worse during the afternoon. By evening, windows were blown out and screen doors were ripped from their hinges. Roofs were torn off neighboring homes and all the animal sheds and the barn at the Nielsens' were blown down.

"I saw the storm tear the outbuildings down one after the other and how the poor horses and cattle ran out into the storm, when they felt their shelter give way." A neighbor's house was literally blown apart, and the family, unable to walk, huddled on the ground outside protecting their faces by turning away from the wind to keep from drowning. The storm did not let up until dawn.

"Never has the church bell sounded so festive to me," Andrea said later, "as that morning when Reverend Madsen rang it. It was as though it said, 'Your children are all well.' And the children came home presently wading in water and mire. Our chickens were drowned . . ."

Her husband was home later and as soon as the land around dried out a bit, the Danes got together for coffee at neighboring homes and decided who needed help and who could give it. "We were like one big family . . ."

Indeed, the Danes were like one big family in the early years, sharing dinners, celebrations on July 4 for United States independence and June 5, the Danish constitution day, and Christmas.

Magdalene Ravn, the wife of Pastor Ravn, thought that Christmas, with the feast and dancing at the community hall, was particularly a children's time. The Danish dance around the tree, the food and the songs were all European, but other things were different.

"Down here the children are not accustomed to looking for Christmas snow each morning when they get up as we used to do in Denmark before Christmas. No, the little Danevang boy, would certainly be surprised if he were to experience a white Christmas. But then he can experience a Christmas with such mild weather that one can have both windows and doors open Christmas Eve, and can see the fireflies light their Christmas lights out on the plains, and maybe see one of those glorious sunsets which is familiar to those who have been where the land is flat and where the horizon can be seen on all sides."

Mrs. Ravn may not have closely observed when Texas fireflies are out, but she remembered well that Nordic Christmas trees were unavailable. The large tree decorating the community hall was actually several native trees tied together in a bundle.

And the children, whose eyes reflected the Christmas tree lights, were not only growing up where there was rarely any snow, but they were also growing up differently. They were doing what later sociologists would call acculturating. They were modifying Danish customs to resemble the larger and somewhat different culture in which they found themselves. Their parents were first generation Danes who were becoming American citizens; they would become Danish Americans who preserved a few older customs; their children would be American.

The first years had been rough, but after all, as a later descendant remarked, "We *are* the sons of Vikings!" The spirit of Danevang was that of the poet Ove Nielsen, who wrote:

> Gone is the Viking who battled the wave
> But never his spirit will rest in the grave.
> We are Americans, fruit of the Danes,
> The blood of the Viking is warm in our veins.

And this was no mere sentiment—it was the truth.

VII.
A New Century

Fewer Danes came to the United States in the early years of the 20 century than in the previous century, but even so they accounted for nearly 90,000 arrivals. Between 1900 and 1914, annual totals rose to almost 7,000 persons.

The first world war almost stopped emigration, but in the 1918 to 1920 period, the number of individuals coming rose again. From 1921 to 1931, about 63,000 Danes left their homeland, but only about half, 34,200, came to the United States. The reason was that after 40 years of debate, the U.S. Congress had finally passed laws regulating European immigration. Also in Denmark, after decades of a prevailing liberalism concerning immigration, the government passed somewhat restrictive policies concerning departures.

In 1921, the first quotas were enacted concerning Denmark. The United States allowed 5,694 Danish immigrants, but this figure proved a bit too high because not that many came. So from 1925, the quota was lowered to 2,789, a figure that proved to be too low. Most of the Danes in excess of the quota chose Canada, and immigration to the United States fell again.

This end of the large immigration figures spelled doom for the use of native Danish in the United States. Fewer and fewer native speakers entered the country, and fewer second generation Danes had any reason to speak Danish. The Ansgar Lutheran Church at Danevang was one of the last places native Danish was used at church services.

After 1900, not only the number, but the character of emigration from Denmark changed. More single men emigrated than those men in families or those counted as children. In the 20 to 30 age group, up to 69% were single men. And the average age of emigrants declined: more people from 20 to 30 years of age came—fewer from the 40 to 60 year old bracket. With the increase of single men came a decline in families, of course. Morever, more individuals came from the cities of Denmark. Some of these people, it is true, had first moved from the country to a Danish town and had stayed there for a time before moving to America. Even so, many urban natives were leaving.

Once in America, the Danes were also going to different places. Most of the earlier Danes settled as farmers—always more spread out than the Norwegian or Swedish families. After the turn of the century Danes chose more often to settle in larger towns, looking for city work.

The central motive for leaving Denmark was usually the same—a lack of opportunity in the homeland. But this reason was now helped along by the railroads in the United States as well as by the established steamship lines and their agents. In fact, steamship company agents were known to go to great lengths to secure passengers. Pastor Erik Moller remembers that at the appearance of Halley's Comet in the skies over Denmark in the spring of 1910, agents maintained that it would miss America but that Denmark was perhaps not so safe. It would therefore be wise to buy a ticket. Moller's family resisted the wild story at the time, but he later made the trip to America, for the more usual reasons.

In the late 19th century, the railroads of the United States were given large amounts of government land somewhat in return for putting in the lines essential for the growth of the new country. At first, there was little profit to a railroad company laying new track in unsettled land. The government gave blocks of public land to the companies as part of their investment. The companies then sold much of this land to settlers. In Denmark many an advertisement appeared offering this land for very cheap prices. And every advertisement claimed to offer the best land.

Emigrant ship at Galveston, 1896

Naturally, the steamship companies still went after the emigrant business. At the turn of the century, a steerage ticket across the Atlantic cost the emigrant $22.50 (not counting food), but the actual cost to the steamship company was about $1.70. It was a profitable business.

In these years, almost 75% of the emigrants traveled on tickets that not only took them across the Atlantic, but also put them aboard a train to land that could be bought or to a city where a job might be had. And the Danes already in America helped matters. Many of the tickets were prepaid for a family member, a prospective bride, farm worker or a friend.

Correspondence between individuals in the United States and Denmark rose dramatically after the turn of the century as did the amount of money sent back to the homeland (to a peak of 2,400,000 kr. in 1911, although some $500,000 came back to the U.S. the same year). A lot of the letters inspired emigration, of course, and some of the money was used to get to America. A few Danes went back home. In the 20th century, perhaps not quite a tenth of the Danes returned. About 8.6% is one estimate.

Emigration figures and statistics usually reflect only the broad outlines of human movement. Statisticians guess that some of the earlier figures concerning emigration and immigration, up to 1870, could be 50% inaccurate. Nobody kept very good records. This error may be trimmed to 10% as one approaches modern times, but whatever the inaccuracies, the figures are indicative of one of the most massive human movements in European history.

The Danes were active immigrants, adding much to this new culture they found—in fact, often directly influencing those around them. In terms of acculturation—the changing patterns of belief and custom and habit—their culture was already Nordic and very similar to the English and other dominant northern European groups they found in America and Texas. In "assimilation"—intermarriage with and being absorbed by other groups—the Danes moved faster than most Norwegians and Swedes.

In dress, Danish clothing was only slightly different from American. Only a few examples of the older regional costumes were brought, as this dress was already uncommon in Denmark.

In farming, methods did differ; but again, the Danes made few efforts to use methods of their old homeland. A common Danish European tradition for farm construction was the habit of constructing dwellings in connected wings. Few followed this style in America, switching to the outbuilding style of the Americans (and Norwegians) which called for separate buildings.

Danish ethnic organizations were similar to other Scandinavian groups, but because there were fewer Danes in a thinner pattern of settlement, they did not last as long. Groups were formed in the Rio Grande valley of Texas and in most large cities. Until the 1930's, Dallas had a coherent group of about 40 Danish families which were later absorbed into other Scandinavian clubs. Other cities, El Paso, Amarillo and Houston, also had a fair number of Danish families that were aware of each other even if lasting organizations were not a result. The Danish Brotherhood in America, still in existence, had chartered groups in Dallas and Galveston in 1912 and 1913. Originally these groups had about 20 charter members from an estimated population of 400 Danes in Dallas and 200 in Galveston. In 1917 the brotherhood counted almost 1300 first generation Danes in Texas and slightly more than 3000 individuals in Texas born of Danish parents.

The Danes of the second generation married outside the group in almost four times greater numbers than the first generation, leading to a fast assimilation in terms of what language was spoken in the home and in family custom. It became difficult to tell just who was to count as a Danish American.

The Danes were inclined not to be too nationalistic. To begin with, some stated their homeland had not offered them enough opportunities or they would never have left. Now that they had left, they were ready to accept another nationality and a new life. Even F. L. Grundtvig, after one of his glowing, nationalistic, colony-creating talks in the midwest, was challenged by an outspoken settler who noted that America gave them food and land while the old country let them go hungry and landless.

Yet the Danes did, for a time, preserve some of their older ways. But they had strong reasons to welcome a new life and little fear of doing so. The Danes were the least nationalistic of any Scandinavian group, and among themselves, most nationalistic only in the Grundtvigian colonies like Danevang.

The evidence of national traits is always questionable, but in literature and letters, the Danes usually characterize themselves as rather modest, unobtrusive people with a notable determination and whimsical humor that can be pronounced in personal relations. They were able to fit in very well in a new land.

Native born Danish settlers in Texas were not very numerous. Between 1850 and 1950, they never numbered more than around one person for every 3,000 of Texas's population. This ratio was about the same for the 1880-1920 period.

The immediate children and later descendants, being born in Texas, are not counted in the earlier census figures. In some counties the school census counted the "descendants." In Williamson County in 1923, for example, one percent of the school children were Danish in descent, much lower than Czech or German, but higher than the second generation Scottish, or Irish, or French. Thus the number of "Danish Texans" in any year is well more than double the recorded numbers:

YEAR	NUMBER OF NATIVE BORN DANISH SETTLERS	% OF TOTAL POPULATION
1940	1117	.017
1930	1350	.023
1920	1508	.032
1910	1287	.033
1900	1089	.036
1890	649	.029
1880	489	.031
1870	159	.019
1860	150	.024
1850	49	.023

County statistics are quite lengthy because many counties list two or three Danes, but by way of comparison, these are the counties reporting 15 or more native born Danes for two decades:

	COUNTY	NUMBER OF NATIVE BORN DANISH SETTLERS
1890	Bexar	38
	Bosque	17
	Dallas	44
	Galveston	61
	Gillespie	22
	Grayson	22
	Harris	25
	Lee	35
	Limestone	24
	McLennan	19
	Milam	18
	Tarrant	15
	Travis	41
	Williamson	20
1900	Bexar	62
	Bosque	22
	Brazoria	42
	Dallas	39
	Denton	17
	Galveston	92
	Gillespie	31
	Grayson	16

Harris	89
Jefferson	33
Lee	17
Limestone	15
McLennan	22
Travis	75
Val Verde	18
Wharton	122
Williamson	89

The figures occasionally reflect errors. The Danes of Lee County, for example, were probably more numerous. The figures do show the appearance of the first settlers at Danevang in Wharton County.

Danes who came to Texas from the turn of the century to about 1930 settled in widely scattered areas, more of them now trying their luck in the cities.

Viggo Kohler, one son of a rather large Copenhagen family, decided that the New World was for him. The family was not poor—the father Frans was in the construction business—but this son was a wanderer. Born in 1844, Viggo was in Chicago by 1867 working first in a box manufacturing plant, then on a bridge building crew. No one in the family now knows why Texas attracted him, but in two years he was in the state. He first settled at St. Mary's of Aransas on Copano Bay. This small port was a well-known lumber import center for west Texas, and Kohler went into that trade. But the area railroad was built into Rockport, St. Mary's declined, and Kohler moved in 1885 to Beeville.

Kohler himself attracted other Danes to Texas, through visits and letters to Denmark. A number of immigrants settled in the area, near the "Viggo Community" including a niece and a nephew, Harold Nielsen. Most of these immigrants were to make Texas their home except for the mother of Viggo's niece. She decided she had had enough of Texas and returned to Denmark.

After 13 years in Beeville, Kohler was attracted both by ranching and land southwest at the railroad stop called Hebbronville. Here, Kohler established himself around 1900. He never married, but adopted a daughter, set up a home and bought land.

His holdings grew to over 35,000 acres, primarily in two ranches. Today, part of the town of Hebbronville stands on land formerly his. In 1915, Kohler built the Viggo Hotel, a landmark for decades. In this year, Hebbronville had only 400 residents, but the hotel hosted ranchers when they were in town, railroad travelers, and local organizations for parties and club meetings. In World War I years, a time of border troubles, it became a stop for military men. When oil became a new area crop around 1928, the hotel expanded. Oil was also found on one of the Kohler ranches.

Kohler maintained strong ties to Denmark, often visiting his family. A grand-daughter, Mrs. Dagmar Cole, remembers that each year Viggo would drape a string of paper Danish flags, the Dannebrog, on the Christmas tree and that a large selection of fruit and cakes would be on hand for visitors. Kohler died in 1930, but by the terms of his will, a home in Denmark was provided as a place of retirement for family members. His descendants operated the hotel, but after a 60-year life, it closed in the 1970's.

It is not known why Kohler left Denmark or why he changed his occupation so many times. But one family recollection is still clear: "To the end of his life he just wanted to do something different."

Viggo Kohler's family in Denmark

Viggo Hotel, Hebbronville

Viggo Kohler

Other Danes tried different parts of the state. J. K. Kristoffersen, a carpenter turned painter, moved to Dallas in 1910 and summed up his emigration experience by saying, "I married one afternoon in the fall of 1910 and we left that same night for Dallas, Texas, U.S.A."

Christian Theodore Ingwersen of Copenhagen came to Houston just before the turn of the century, married Miss Rogilla Murdock of Alabama and moved to Nederland. He worked there for the Texas Company for 12 years.

Paul Jenson of Hals, Jylland, followed his brother to Denver, Colorado, around 1915 to set up a dairy business. Within five years he was at Borger, Texas, with his own dairy. In later years, he became superintendent of a creamery at Pampa, met and married a Texas girl, Nell Roach, and established his family. For a time, Jenson set up his own dairy at Hereford. By 1941, he was in partnership with Vigo Paterson in the Wayne Milk Company of Littlefield, where he stayed until his retirement.

In Galveston, where some of the incoming Danes stopped, Hans Guldmann made a fortune after his arrival in 1907. His first business was dealing in cottonseed products, but he also served on many boards of directors, the Galveston Wharf Company, local banks and the Hotel Galvez Company. For many years, Guldmann was Danish consul at Galveston. In 1932, however, Guldmann was found shot in his bathroom, perhaps a victim of the depression years, although the investigating justice ruled the shooting in the right side of his head as accidental.

John N. Christensen and A. Johan Rasmussen started what was to become Galveston's first automobile dealership when they opened a bicycle shop at the turn of the century. Rasmussen came to New York in 1890 from Horsens, Jylland, when he was 20 years old but did not like the climate. He moved to Galveston in 1893 to get away from the cold.

Christensen arrived in the United States, the family later said, "speaking a foreign tongue, friendless, and with only $16 in his pocket." The $16 had evidently been earned as a farmhand in Nebraska where he first came from Lemvig, Jylland. To learn English, Christensen kept his pockets stuffed with newspaper clippings which he reread at every opportunity. In this way, he learned to read English in three months and was a fluent speaker in two years. Railroad advertisements for land brought him to Texas, but in Galveston, he met A. J. Rasmussen who was not only a countryman, but also assured the new arrival that a bicycle shop would be profitable.

According to Rasmussen, the revenue from "swains with a penchant for taking their loves bicycle riding" would support a small company. Rasmussen had the swains of Galveston figured correctly. The rental of "bicycles built for two" netted them $10 on weekdays and $20 on Sundays. From this start, the pair went on to sporting goods, then automobiles in 1904. Rasmussen said that the early auto drivers had little confidence in the new machines, and most of the driving during the first years was done on the beach. Christensen also liked Galveston because of the sea—he had missed it in mid-continent living.

Other Galveston Danes moved to the mainland and a number set themselves up as truck farmers in Brazoria County near Liverpool along Chocolate Bayou.

They were typical examples. In these years, Danes were moving into all areas of the state. Some even tried high plains farming.

A. J. Rasmussen

In the spring of 1907, Harry Sorrenson, his wife, Bertha, and their daughter, Effie Mae, left Iowa to make their home in Texas. Harry was the son of Andrew and Katrina Sorrenson, who had come from Hals, Jylland, to the United States.

Harry had been born in Illinois, lived with his parents there and in Iowa, married Bertha Nelson, a Norwegian girl, and had decided he had had enough of the northern climate. He made the trip to Texas twice before moving his family, once to secure land and once again, with his Swedish friend Pete Peterson, to build sheds, fences and corrals for farm animals, to get a well dug, and to start construction on a house.

In 1907, the entire family boarded a train for the trip south. Sorrenson had bought a parcel of land from a company that had an agreement with a railroad to bring in the possessions of the purchaser and his family, free. Harry rode the box car most of the way from Iowa to Swisher County with his horses, cows, pigs, chickens, household goods and furniture, clothing, a pump organ, black-smith forge and anvil tools, camera equipment and a carefully packed violin. He took care of the livestock, while Bertha took care of her daughter in the passenger car.

The load was a bit unusual. Sorrenson was himself exceptional. As far as official schooling went, he had a third grade education. But at 33, he was not only a competent farmer but also a proficient mathematician, was widely read, had a hobby of photography from his teenage years and was a metal worker.

Arriving in Tulia, the family unloaded and spent their first night at the White Hotel. The next day the family rode their wagon to the farm of the Bookout family, where they were to stay while Harry finished their own home. This was soon done, and the family set up house in their new residence.

Harry soon found that as the only photographer around, he had ample opportunities for meeting new friends. Invitations to Sunday dinners were frequent—with the request that the camera be brought along also. Harry charged only for the materials and soon had a sideline occupation and many friendships. He took photographs of families, group outings, farm scenes and even several of people after death when the family had no other pictures of the recently deceased. In the early years, he used glass negatives and accumulated so many he built a greenhouse with them.

Harvest on the Sorrenson farm, Swisher County, Texas, 1920

Sorrenson children in the family kitchen, Swisher County, 1910

Bertha Sorrenson and children on a visit to a neighbor's farm, Swisher County, 1912

Danish visitors at Sorrenson's in 1913: Peter and Karen Petersen, Katrina and Andrew Sorrenson

Harry and Bertha Sorrenson, 1937

The family soon grew to four children: Effie Mae, Ernest, Doris and Grace.

Life on the plains of Texas was not quite what they had expected. The land was indeed warmer than the north country, but in some years, too dry. When the feed crops for the livestock failed, Sorrenson and his neighbors would have to truck in hay, leaving their families alone for days at a time.

And the Texas northers—for shorter times—seemed worse than the Iowa cold. Harry built a mule-drawn cart for his children to use for transportation to the school, which was three miles away. This was a short distance in good weather, but with a norther coming in, it was dangerous to try to walk that far across a countryside that afforded little protection. A later visit to Iowa made one thing clear: the Texas panhandle was home, the family really did not want to go back.

Bertha not only worked at keeping up with the family's clothes and cooking, but also helped out in the fields, particularly during harvest. When she was in the fields, one of the children would climb up on the "chip house" and wave a white dish towel at regular intervals to indicate there was nothing wrong. If this signal did not regularly appear, Bertha would hurry home. The "chip house," by the way, was just that. It was a shed for storing cow manure which was the summer fuel for the cook stove in a land with a lack of plentiful wood. And chips were especially good summer fuel. They would produce a hot fire, but one that died quickly, leaving the kitchen comparatively cool.

With such fuel, Bertha could cook up a meal so good that some of the threshing crew said that anyone would work for the Sorrensons for the meals alone. In addition, Bertha sometimes served as a midwife to neighboring women and as veterinarian for a sick animal. It was a country where one either rose to the occasion or did without.

The C. J. Vars family bought land quite close to the Sorrensons and the families became friends. The men helped each other with the farm work, even owning some equipment in common. The women cooked together for the threshing crews. The Vars had come from New York, and since neither family had close relatives, they spent Christmas with each other.

The families would get together for outings, buggy rides, and even shared the same post office box at Tulia. However, the family dogs hated each other. The Vars's bulldog and the Sorrensons's shepherd would, every visit, go for each other and would end up in a tangle. At this point, Vars and Sorrenson would walk over, grab the hind legs of their respective animals and ceremoniously carry them to a convenient stock tank and throw them in. That would end the fight for the day.

Both Bertha and Harry liked music. With Harry playing the violin and Bertha the organ, there was no lack of music in the home. Harry even had an Edison cylinder phonograph recorder and recorded some home musical sessions.

The main troubles the family had concerned the years of drought. There were others. After 1913, the farmers in the area were told they did not have clear title to their lands because of an earlier, faulty survey. This resulted in everyone actually owning part of whoever's land was to the north. The Sorrensons had 20 acres left on which their improvements stood, when their land was suddenly legally the property of the landowner south of them. Most farmers were reluctant to move and did as Harry did: bought his farm for the second time and stayed on the land.

In 1937, Harry and Bertha were named "Master Farmers of Swisher County" by the farm extension service. By this time they had also achieved another goal—raising their children, providing for their education, and seeing them off on careers of their own: the girls were teachers before and after their marriages and the son went into farming himself.

Harry died in 1962 at 89 and Bertha died in 1967, leaving four children, eight grandchildren and sixteen great-grandchildren as a Texas family.

Family reunion of the Lloyd Bentsen Sr., family at McAllen   *Peter Bentsen*

Peter Bentsen and his family took one of the usual routes to Texas—by way of the midwest—but moved far south, the lower Rio Grande Valley, and founding a large family.

Peter emigrated to the United States in 1884 when he was 19. After a look at San Francisco, he decided on South Dakota as a good place to settle. There were other Danes nearby in a loose colonial setting with other families including Germans, Norwegians and Swedes.

A lack of land, and no financial future for the young man, turned him into an emigrant. In Denmark, Peter's father leased farmland and worked a six day week: three days for the landowner, three for himself. The family was at times short of both food and money. Once, Peter's father had found a wild goose frozen to the ice. He brought it home. Half of that goose became a Christmas dinner and the other half was sold for a welcome two kroner.

In 1889, Peter married Tena Petersen, who had come with her family from Viborg. Her parents, Anton and Hanna, had seen notices in Danish newspapers advertising Dakota lands. The advertisements alluded to Dakota gold, but the land itself was enough to make the move worthwhile. As a provision of the United States Homestead Act, a family could receive a quarter section, 160 acres, free—if 20 acres were farmed and developed. The government—and the railroads—were trying to fill up the land with settlers.

The new land was an opportunity, but the life there was hard. A youngster like Lloyd Bentsen, the third child of the couple, was milking cows as a regular chore at four years of age and harvesting and plowing at six. Even Tena worked in the fields in addition to her housework. Work extended at the very least from sunup to sundown.

In the Dakotas, severe winters were common. A cord was strung outside between house and barn to follow during days of blowing snow. And the first "house" was a pit dug in the earth, covered with sod and timbers. But it was their home and it was all theirs. Peter felt so strongly about his new homeland that he did not allow Danish spoken in the home—English only—and the family attended the "American" church, not the local Danish Lutheran.

In spite of these efforts, Lloyd was called a "damn foreigner" once at school. His mother, assuring him that he was just as American as anyone else born in the country, gave him an answer by saying that "a foreigner is only the man who came after the man who came before, everyone is a foreigner except the Indians." And from his father, Lloyd heard the feeling inspired from experience in Denmark: "Get ahold of all the land you can, and hang on."

Peter made a success of his farm and eventually built up an estate worth $100,000, the equivalent of a million dollars today. But about this time, Texas became an attraction. Peter had journeyed south once, interested by the land promotion of John H. Shary, and liked what he saw. Peter immediately bought ten acres and gave a great deal of thought to northern winters. In the Valley, he had seen "strawberries and roasting ears at Christmas time," and had noticed what he thought were better crops growing in the south Texas winter than in a Dakota spring.

Near the end of World War I, in June of 1918, Peter moved to Texas, built a house and founded a nursery. Other family members followed. Lloyd, already in the army in Texas, came to visit, met his future wife, Edna Ruth Colbath, and ended up staying and marrying.

In the early 1900's, Valley land was scrub land with a few exceptions like John Shary's first efforts at citrus orchards. But the land around McAllen and Mission had a future. Lloyd started out by clearing land for others, then began buying land for himself. A man who learned to back his own judgment, he also realized one must have the right breaks. During the depression, Lloyd had a friend willing to loan him $30,000 without note or collateral. He found 5000 acres for the price, at $6 an acre, low in cost even then. In four years, Lloyd Bentsen had turned the property for two million dollars—this from a young man who had $1.50 in his pocket when he married. By the end of World War II, Lloyd and his brother Elmer controlled 100,000 acres of land and were known as prominent businessmen and ranchers.

Lloyd M. Bentsen Jr., one of a group of notable Bentsens, has carried on the family tradition by becoming a successful Houston businessman and United States Senator. In fact, the Bentsen family has 114 lineal descendants, all in a 100 year span, a true Danish Texan dynasty.

And in the first third of the century, another Dane tried what might have been, or might be, the last colonization effort in central Texas, but not particularly for Danes.

John B. Christensen, a second-generation Danish American, came to Dallas around 1913. He left a career in Missouri as an attorney and worked through a wide assortment of jobs including speculation in railroads, paved toll road construction for the new automobiles, sawmill work and farming. He married a 16-year-old east Texas girl during the sawmill-operator period and more or less settled down in the community of Rainbow near Glen Rose in 1922 as a land promoter, town developer, editor of the *Rainbow Reminder*, general store owner and toll road builder.

Christensen had developed a number of curious dreams along the way: a system of hard surfaced roads for Texas, a series of dams to provide power and water, a rural electricity distribution system and an industrial-agricultural community.

The latter was attempted. On New Years Day 1928, Christensen contracted for the purchase of the De Cordova Bend land, about 6000 acres, for a promised $120,000 in deferred payments. This was land in a deep loop of the Brazos River, heavily timbered and fertile, where Jacob de Cordova tried, and failed in the 1860's, to establish a textile manufacturing center.

Christensen called the place Kristenstad, "Kristen's town." News of the effort got around, particularly in Dallas and Ft. Worth, and settlers started coming. Christensen interested them in purchasing land at $40 an acre—with no down payment and a cow included in the deal. He at first wanted all Scandinavian families, but desirable buyers appeared from many back-grounds. The families who wanted to purchase the land were carefully interviewed and told about the philosophy of the community. A news writer of the day said: "These people did not come here to build a city, and thus repeat the age-old experiment, that groans aloud with its unemployed and its im-poverished. They came here because they had faith in the ideals upon which this settlement is founded—that everyone should own his own land and be as nearly self-supporting as possible."

Gradually, the community took on the aspect of a cooperative venture as corporations were formed to handle group marketing and purchasing. Christensen was careful to say that there was not a touch of communism or socialism in the operation. The only "-ism" he would say, "is Americanism."

The effort was well planned. Trees that were cleared were cut up in a local sawmill for lumber; the scraps of this operation went to a chair factory which turned out straight and rocking chairs with cowhide bottoms (the hides from local cows); the scrap from the chair factory went to a charcoal mill; and the charcoal was sold to railroads and stores. The activities separate from farming were carried out by community members on a volunteer, paid basis as they had spare time from raising crops or taking care of livestock. Families were encouraged to produce everything they needed first, then produce for profit.

John B. Christensen at Kristenstad in the 1930's

Community products were milk and eggs, cedar posts, peanuts and pigs. Local wild grapes were turned into marketable juice and even the young people had what was called "the children's business." They were kept busy gathering certain flowers, roots, herbs and bark. These were sold for the preparation of drugs and cosmetics.

The community even issued its own currency: die stamped "checks" of brass in five, ten, twenty-five and fifty cent denominations. These could be earned through volunteer work in the community businesses or the sale of surplus farm products through the marketing association and could be used to buy supplies at the local store.

By 1933, about 40 families lived in the bend, about 200 people, in a variety of homes ranging from dugouts to stone dwellings. There was a post office and community hall building which served as school, library and non-sectarian church. One building contained a print shop which turned out a local magazine, *The Interpreter.*

The colony soon found itself with a curious reputation as a Utopia—a term largely spawned in over-zealous newspaper stories by outsiders but hotly denied by Christensen. One story pointed out more correctly that the community "is not a refuge for the impractical sentimentalist, nor is it the mango growth of fanatics." Even the *New York Times* hailed the creation of the innovative colony.

C. M. Hammond, writing in *The Texas Weekly* in 1931, painted a fairly accurate picture but certainly a complimentary one. He said that Kristenstad was "merging industry with agriculture and striving to make of itself the ideal community of the future."

"If Texas ever is to be the prosperous independent State it should be," Hammond continued, "every one of its communities and towns must attain something like the ideal of Kristenstad."

Naturally, such words would interest people in times of increasing financial difficulty, for the depression years were at hand. Banks failed and urban jobs were impossible to find. The colony attracted two types of settlers: subsistence farmers and a group of artisans, professors and poets. The latter, even as conditions slid into a nationwide depression, became disillusioned and not at all happy with their return to nature. The former found themselves at times unable to market their crops and facing a local drought. The chair factory burned and there was no money to rebuild.

John B. Christensen Sr.

Dissension spread through the colony. Christensen took care of some people out of his own pocket, but his funds were not sufficient to underwrite the effort. Even a well-intentioned bid for Federal aid by a Dallas friend failed and brought criticism on the colony.

Many of the settlers left, and even Christensen moved back to Rainbow with his family, where he suddenly died in 1937. The bulk of the land, never paid off, reverted to the heirs of the earlier owners.

Most of Christensen's "wild ideas" soon became realities: a statewide paved highway system, flood control and a constant water supply from reservoirs, and a rural electrical system. But only the memory of a Kristenstad survived.

VIII.
"Is There Nothing Left from the Good Old Days?"

After the 1930's, modern times came to Danevang—as to most places in Texas. Texas was moving into the urban period and times were changing.

A few years before, a newcomer to Danevang could still expect strange things. When N. P. Hald came to Danevang as a minister in 1928, he did not know what to expect:

"I thought, as so many of the Danes in the North, that the climate in Texas was too severe for us Northerners, and that we might be both cooked and fried. Perhaps, I too had a secret fear that we then might be eaten by Negroes and Mexicans; but that fear I was too smart to speak of to anyone." But Hald, in that year, was pleased because Danish was still used in the colony, certainly most of the time at the church.

Hald, once in Danevang, thoroughly liked the little colony. He attended Den danske Kvindeforening, the Danish ladies' church league, where the songs were as good as the coffee—and "gossip was neither heard nor spoken." During these years some services were held in English "for the benefit of the young people and for any Americans who might wish to come." But although the minister distinguished between Americans and the Danes of Danevang, the Danes themselves were becoming Americans.

In 1934 a new pastor, A. E. Frost, and his wife Emma moved to Danevang, and they commented on the settlement in a slightly different way. They were new to the south, but not to Danes, and were happy to find themselves among countrymen. They were delighted with the parsonage and its newly installed "electric lights and water works." But that evening they heard the "midnight dance of the fourfooted,"—the rats on the ceiling. They planted trees nearby, conducted all the church meetings, and considered the problem of whether to give services in English or not. "According to an old saying, the gnome moves along. So did the language problem. Was it possible to preserve the content of our Danish heritage," mused the pastor, "without retaining the language?"

The minister noted also that Grundtvig's plan for other colonies had not materialized. Although some Danes did move to other southern states, the group in Granly, Mississippi, was still the nearest colony of Danes. In Texas, except for some families like the area of "Little Denmark" in Lee County, Danevang was isolated. The young people were taking their acquaintances, and even husbands and wives, from the people around them. And the people around them were not Danes. Then, many of the younger families were moving away. In 1923, there were 97 Danish families in the community. By 1927, the population of Danevang was over 500, but declining.

The solution about the language was not long in coming: English was introduced in church. The older people met also with the younger at the English services and some of the younger met at the Danish service. But the question was really a one-sided contention—Danish was used less and less.

Rev. Frost observed that "it was quite an experience for me to take part in the community's cooperative enterprises, which were earning quite a name for Danevang far and wide. It was interesting to see how the second generation took over the works after their fathers. Will the third generation also have that understanding and interest in those enterprises?"

For some individuals the answer was no. The trees the pastor planted stayed put, but many of the younger people did not. Quite a few of the second generation took over the business of the colony, but most of the third generation moved away.

The 1930's saw the contention between the "old men" and the "young men" of the community. The board of the cooperative society was taken over by the second generation, and the first pioneers, the older fathers and mothers, came to be advisors of the future. But the second generation was as successful.

The community gin processed 4138 bales of cotton in 1930 and just the next year, 5323. By 1937, a second gin was acquired at Midfield and by 1941, "outsiders" were accepted as cooperative members in the Danish organization. By the 1950's, 8,000 bale seasons were common. Other crops became prominent, particularly feed grains and rice.

In 1935 at the synod's annual convention, J. C. Evers visited Danevang for the last time. He had seen the colony achieve successful days. F. L. Grundtvig had died in 1903 in Denmark, still remembered for his lectures, dramatic readings

Carl Jensen family and home at Danevang

P. J. Petersen with his children

A croquet game in Danevang

Danevang confirmation class in 1908

The Petersen family on a corn wagon, Danevang

Highway through Danevang, c. 1924

Mr. and Mrs. J. P. Olson and daughters at Danevang, 1922

*Wedding of Michael Mikkelsen and Elna
Petersen in Danevang, c. 1923*

Cotton bales at Danevang

Ruins of the Danevang church after the 1945 storm

Anniversary meeting of the Danish Ladies' Aid
Society, Danevang, c. 1930

Danish Day gathering at the community hall, Danevang

Danish Day meal at Danevang

The Danish Ladies' Aid Society, Danevang, 1971

Danish Day at the community hall, Danevang

The dance around the community
Christmas tree, Danevang

and songs when he visited the young colony. But Danevang had achieved its goal, even if change was under way. Individuals from all parts of Denmark had joined and made a go of a colony. Their minister had even visited the Hutto, Texas, group of Danes, and that area had traded settlers with Danevang such as Søren Jensen Westergaard and Marie Westergaard who came from Denmark to Hutto in 1889 and moved to Danevang in 1911. A few Danes from other towns—Houston, Galveston and Dallas—arrived between 1897 and about 1911. Danevang also attracted Danes directly from Denmark: Hans N. Berndt came in 1905, Fritz and Anne Hansen came in 1908. Laurits Lauritsen moved from Schleswig in 1921, and Carl Thyssen arrived in 1909 from his home near Toftlund in north Schleswig.

Other than celebrations such as Independence Day and Christmas, the Danes got together for birthdays and Sunday dinners, card games and anniversaries, amateur theatrical performances and readings, always with good food and lots of singing. When homes were built, the traditional wreath of boughs and flowers was placed right above the door and the community was full of Danish folk tales and stories, certainly always those of Hans Christian Andersen. Mrs. Ella Hansen, then one of the Olson children, remembers that her father's stories would move the children to laughter—and tears.

And before World War II, Danevang even maintained a 40-piece band that played benefits for highway construction and the building of Camp Hulen.

The ministers, for all of the obvious Danish amazement over the blacks who took odd jobs in the community, could never understand why, in the 1930's, "Texas forbids two races to congregate under one public roof." The Danes had been taught that the church and state were separate, and any race was welcome in St. Ansgar's.

The first church, finished and dedicated in 1909, was destroyed by a hurricane in 1945 and a second one was built, from an army chapel building, in 1947. A new parsonage was built in 1949, the first mechanical cotton picker arrived in 1948, the schools were finally consolidated with El Campo in 1951, and the first non-Danish pastor arrived in 1968. All-English services had been started in 1954, but some Danish hymns are still sung today, particularly at holiday times. About the language in church, Johanne Petersen probably answered Rev. Rost well enough when she said, "The Sunday School and vacation school have gone over to the English but are none the less valuable for that." In the later years, the only church services conducted in Danish were occasional funerals and baptisms. Some baptisms were for Houston families, first-generation Danes who could find no closer Danish-speaking pastor.

There were always a few bad years. Indeed, the storm of 1945 that destroyed the church dumped some 20 inches of rain on the settlement and turned it into a lake deep enough to float cotton bales away from the gin.

During one flood, a couple of men on the north side of the settlement got in their small boat used for fishing on the coast and sailed a few miles south to visit friends. They sailed right up to the porch and tied their boat to one of the gallery posts.

A fall festival, common among Grundtvigian Danes, was one of the customs of the colony for many years. They were church-related but involved many activivies and were, originally, just over a week in length.

Usually, a pastor from some other part of the country would be invited as a speaker—and an exhausting schedule he had. The week started with a Sunday service, then a meeting that afternoon and each following afternoon through Friday. Every meeting was centered around a talk by the pastor, usually on a religious topic, or a presentation by a second guest on other topics. Agriculturalists or college professors might be invited to speak. In any case, each meeting was followed by a "coffee-table" at the community hall—a large selection of coffee cakes and coffee. In the evenings, meetings would be held at the homes of various individuals, and these would involve perhaps an informal talk, a story reading, much visiting, a selection of songs, and many sandwiches and coffee.

Saturday, no meetings were held, but an outing was. Most of the community, with the speakers and guests, would go for a day-long picnic to the 20 acres of church-owned grounds distant about four miles on Tres Palacios Creek, or a fishing trip to the coast would be organized.

Sunday would bring a repeat of the services, and the week would be at an end. The festival weeks were initially very popular, perhaps because there were no movie theaters or television sets, as Mrs. Louise Petersen remarked much later. In the earlier years, the festival was considered almost "a necessary condition for living." Later with more individual diversions, the festival declined first to a two-day affair and is at present not held.

During World War II, young men from Danevang not only served in the armed forces, but also the children performed folk dances at Camp Hulen, near the coast.

But by the third generation, most of the older ways of life were gone. Young children rode the school bus to El Campo and when they grew up, many moved away. The descendants no longer know Danish and do not make quite as much point of being the sons of Vikings as did their grandfathers.

In April of 1971, the last meeting of Den danske Kvindeforening was held. This Danish-speaking and Danish-titled ladies' league of the local church had been organized in 1900 to help the church, the Bible school and foreign missions. The organization had provided for furnishings, including communion cups, candelabra, the pulpit and an organ. Church and community hall repairs

The church and community hall at Danevang

Aerial view of Danevang, 1950's

Harold A. Hansen of Danevang (1897-1971), civic leader, board member of several cooperative associations, charter member of the Wharton County Junior College Board and builder of an outstanding private collection of items from Danevang's past

The "Danish Field," church and community hall at Danevang in distance

were sponsored, a sidewalk was paid for, stoves were bought and books were purchased for summer school. The society even gave a gift in 1923 to the King and Queen of Denmark for their silver anniversary.

From 1939 on, however, the society had been gradually replaced by a younger, English-speaking group of church ladies. The meeting was like those of the past, but with no new business and more food. Pastor Moller read the traditional story in Danish, songs were sung, and the final minutes were read—perhaps the last time native Danish was officially used in Texas.

Yet, some of the original spirit remains in the community. The Danish Day dinner is occasionally held, attracting bus loads of Scandinavian club members from larger cities for a typical Danish meal. And the Christmas celebration remains Danish in part. The decorated tree at the community hall, now an imported northern tree, is still the center for circles of dancers. The inner circle is the youngest—now mostly the grandchildren and greatgrandchildren brought "home" for a visit—and the outer rings are the older members, the last of the second generation Danes. One or two songs are still sung in Danish. The traditional *Nu har vi Jul igen* is sung faster and faster as the people circle until the sudden entrance of a somewhat Americanized "Santa Claus" delights everyone. He carries a large sack of fruits and candy for the young children. The Americanization may be an improvement. Only the family cat can see Julenissen, Santa Claus's Danish twin.

And around the walls of the community hall, where Danish coffee and pastries, the aeblekage and brunekager, are in abundance, one can still hear talk even from the young men, many living with their families in Bay City and Houston, now proud to be Danish.

It is a strange thing in the history of immigrants and their families that usually the third generation looks with renewed interest on their heritage. Perhaps the first generation and their children had more of a struggle or worked harder at becoming citizens of the land they newly called home.

Many years ago, P. J. Agerskov Petersen wrote his wish that "may the young people, who are entering the ranks where the old ones gradually fall out," continue with the fall festival, the church, school and work "and also in the folk-life! May the Danish language never die out here on the plains!"

Many of the younger people left, the fall festival ceased, but not all had died out. And some descendants have even moved back. At the present time, some 20 younger families (sons and daughters in the third and fourth generation) have returned as farmers to the Danevang area.

Times have changed, of course. The first farmers held land in 40, 80 or 120 acre size most commonly. Today, a family may cultivate thousands of acres. Farming has become mechanized. Pastor Erik Moller, now retired to his former pastorate, thinks "it is a tragedy that our industrial society has lost sight of the values of the small community." And that is true. Danevang, as a Danish American colony, was impossible to maintain as much because of economics as "Americanism." No ono today can make a profit on 40 acres in competition with huge farms. Many people think this a sad thing. Most small farm communities ceased to be, and Danevang, one of them, only happened to be a Danish colony.

Even so, the descendants are still on the coastal plain of Danevang.

So there is an answer to the question written by P. J. Agerskov Petersen for the 50th anniversary of Danevang in 1944:

Er der ikke Spor tilbage
fra de gode, gamle Dage?
Er der mon et lille Minde,
om en enkelt Mand og Kvinde?

Is there nothing left whatever
from the good, old days?
Is there, I wonder, a small reminder
of any single man or woman?

And the answer is yes.

IX.
Recent Emigration

Danish emigration changed drastically in the decades after World War II. For the first time, Danish emigration outstripped Swedish or Norwegian. From 1956 to 1969, 36,798 Danes left their homeland, compared to 11,363 Norwegians and 18,280 Swedes. But only about a quarter (28%) of this number came to the United States. Most of them, nearly half (40%), settled in Canada, while about an eighth (12%) settled in New Zealand and Australia. In the United States, Los Angeles and Chicago became the largest urban centers of Danish settlement.

In 1969 and 1970, fewer than 1000 Danes came each year to the United States and in the 30 years after World War II, the number of first and second generation Danes—as recorded by the United States census—peaked and declined. People of Danish heritage naturally increased—there was no effective way to count these.

After World War II, travel between Denmark and the Americas resumed. Several Danes visited Texas and left a few comments on the area.

Knud Clauson-Kaas visited Texas in 1946 and 1947 and a year later published *Vi ruller gennem Amerika* (Rolling through the States). He knew about Danevang before planning his trip and had even heard it called a "model colony." The visit was not a disappointment.

Clauson-Kaas and his daughter were rather enthusiastic about Texas and knew by the surroundings when they neared Danevang. Although the neat houses with gardens were not typically Danish in construction, the manner in which they were kept showed that Danes lived there. And some of the interiors were quite Danish.

The visitors drove around the Texas settlement, visited with many of the families, but made a telling observation: the young people were leaving to live elsewhere, although for particular celebrations they would return.

Georg Andersen, writing *Dette forbløffende Amerika* (This Amazing America) a little later in the 1940's, remarks more critically of the state and its obvious racial prejudice. He was particularly fond of drive-in movies, amused by mailboxes that were labeled "City—Texas—Other States and Foreign Countries," and refers to Sam Houston as a "Texican," in a relatively rare modern use of the term. He also was amazed at how recent all the history was, commenting that 1836 was not very long ago, but hardly refers to local Danes.

Across the United States, the Danish Lutheran churches (except for about two), dropped the adjective "Danish," and most services were now held in English. For all the Scandinavian languages, certainly Swedish, Norwegian and Danish, the same joke was told about the old-timer who would say "Certainly we use English every day, but if we don't teach the children Danish, what will they do when they get to heaven?" But in another generation this was no longer even a joke.

Today, there are no large Danish organizations in Texas. The Danish Brotherhood, a fraternal-insurance group now nationwide, has no lodges in Texas. It once did, with organizations in Dallas and Houston just after World War I.

Houston is the present location of a Danish consulate, and there is also an honorary royal consul in Dallas. Houston, attracting Danish ships and businessmen, is the more active area.

One of the well-known consuls in Houston was Bernhard Daugbjerg. Born in Jylland in 1904, Daugbjerg grew up to be a member in the royal guard. Thereafter, however, he decided to leave and try his fortune elsewhere. He first landed in Florida where he worked as an awning maker while he learned English and made very little money. He then came to Houston to stay. He said later he "didn't have enough money to go any farther."

But in Houston, he found his home. He became a citizen and joined the Wyatt C. Hedrick Engineering Corporation, a firm he was to work with for 30 years and retire from as a vice-president.

He married Emmylou Boenker and became prominent in local affairs. Daugbjerg was a long-time member of the Houston Chamber of Commerce, an organizer of the Houston Scandinavian Club and the leader in many a local civic concern.

As honorary Danish consul, he drew no salary, but put in countless hours hosting visiting Danes, seeing to their problems and concerning himself with local Danish settlers.

Christmas Eve, for the consul, was not a time to be home with the family but rather the time to visit the crews of Danish ships in the Port of Houston with a kind word and a bit of cheer.

Daugbjerg made many trips to Denmark before his death in 1971 and even held the Danish rank of Knight in the 17th century Order of the Dannebrog, conferred by King Frederick IX in 1966. But when asked if he would return to Denmark he said, "Texas always will be my home."

Another two Danish descendants, father and son, made Texas their temporary and permanent home, respectively. Gutzon Borglum was born near the Nevada-Idaho border in 1867. His father, Dr. James de la Mothe Borglum was a Danish emigrant who had given up woodcarving for medicine and had found his future in the post-Civil War west.

It was a wild place, but young John Gutzon de la Mothe Borglum grew up on a mixture of Danish legends, Dante, Socrates, and stories of the Crow and Sioux nations. He also grew up, after study in California and France, as an accomplished painter and sculptor with a flair for heroic size. His years in the western United States gave Borglum experiences with things western—which affected his later work. Soon he was taking commissions for military statuary and personal busts.

After a legendary row with irate members of the Stone Mountain Confederate Monumental Association over who was to do what work on the Memorial to the Confederacy at Stone Mountain, Georgia, the equally irate Borglum was attracted to Texas. After destroying his models for the mountain-sized job, he literally left Georgia just ahead of the sheriff. During his travels, Borglum had seen Texas, and in 1926, with his wife Mary, son Lincoln and daughter Mary Ellis, he decided on the state for what he came to call his adopted home. He had already become involved in the fantastic idea to carve four giant heads in the South Dakota granite hills and decided to commute there from Texas.

Borglum liked Texas. He was always attracted to the large and made San Antonio his home. He moved into the Menger Hotel in 1927 and used a deserted warehouse in town as a studio. He was to stay in the state 15 years.

Borglum divided his time between Texas and the Mount Rushmore project. While in the state he had three rooms at the Menger Hotel decorated as an apartment and established a more permanent studio in an old stone pumphouse in Brackenridge Park. It was city property, but he secured permission to remodel the structure and work there. Five foot models of the heads for the Rushmore project were done, these at one-twelveth size. Borglum executed the North Carolina State Memorial at Gettysburg, General John

Greenway's statue for Arizona, a bronze of Woodrow Wilson as commissioned by Paderewski for Poland (later melted down by Nazi forces for shell casings), and a portrait of Sidney Lanier for the Washington Memorial Library, among many others. When Major Gordon W. Lillie, "Pawnee Bill," and wild-west-show partner of Buffalo Bill, came to the Texas studio to sit for his bust, Borglum's place filled up with admiring youngsters.

Gutzon Borglum

Work on Washington's nose, Black Hills Monument, South Dakota

The years were full of commissions. Borglum's fame, with major works in the United States and many European countries, was international. He visited Denmark in 1931, received the Order of the Dannebrog, and successfully tried out his rather dated Danish. He still could speak the language he had learned from his father.

Yet Borglum was offered little work in Texas. He did attend meetings of the Trail Drivers Association and was engaged to do a monument which is now in front of the memorial building next to the Witte Museum in San Antonio. But other work for Texas never came to pass. Borglum designed an outdoor theater for Brackenridge Park that was rejected by the city, his designs for the Corpus Christi bay front area were not approved as a WPA project, and of the 40 sculptural commissions granted by Texas for the centennial of its independence, Borglum received none.

The Mount Rushmore project took more and more of his time. Borglum was convinced—as he was about many of his works—that it would be a truly national memorial of the United States and a legacy for eternity. The project, and perhaps the lack of job offers in Texas, drew him away from his adopted

Gutzon Borglum and bust of Lincoln

The Black Hills Monument, South Dakota

Model for the Corpus Christi bayfront project,
planned by Borglum but never constructed

Lincoln Borglum at work on a model

Lincoln Borglum (seated) and Gutzon Borglum
confer about a project

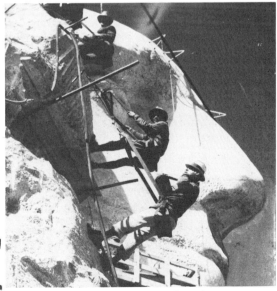

Gutzon Borglum at work on the
Black Hills project

state. He chose California, where he had spent part of his youth and where he had first actually practiced his art. Borglum, however, continued to be interested in and irritated by Texas. During the centennial of 1936, he wrote many letters to government and civic leaders in Texas (which occasionally found their way to various newspapers) generally damning the quality of sculpture, and the planning behind it, done for the celebration.

One thing Borglum did—almost always—was to speak his mind freely. He was still writing letters in 1940 when he was elected a member of the Philosophical Society of Texas. On that occasion, he wrote a two-page, single-spaced letter condemning the way Texas had presented its heroes in stone and bronze. He called the works "frightful, aesthetic failures," not completely attributable to the "so-called artists," but also to the fault of the commissioners dealing with the funds. Then he added a postscript accepting the society membership "with very great pleasure."

Only once perhaps, did Borglum keep his mouth diplomatically shut. While working on the bay front design for Corpus Christi, he took an automobile trip to New York. He had, in the spirit of newly acquired civic pride, pasted a chamber of commerce sticker on his windshield.

Going down Fifth Avenue, perhaps with his mind on the 32 foot statue of Christ the Man he planned, Borglum ran a red light. An Irish policeman soon had him stopped by the curb. As the policeman walked up, however, his eye was caught by the "Corpus Christi" in bold display on the windshield. The policeman smiled and tipped his hat, saying, "Sure an' it's all right father, but don't do it again. Even a priest can get killed by such recklessness."

Gutzon Borglum's life was filled with more than painting and sculpture. He was a gifted writer as well as an operator of a bus line in Stamford, Connecticut, his home for many years. While in Connecticut in 1918, he hosted Czechoslovak freedom fighters and helped write the Czechoslovakian constitution with Jan Masaryk, son of the new country's first president. He was also a sponsor of roadside beautification in Texas many years later.

Borglum, living first in Texas then in California, brought the massive Mount Rushmore job almost to completion. He worked under government financing most of the time and was often exasperated with the demands for advance budgets, job descriptions, work schedules and progress reports—all of which he felt were unnecessary for a great work of art.

Gutzon Borglum died at the end of the 15 year project in May of 1941, leaving his son Lincoln to finish the task by October of that year.

Lincoln had done a lot of growing up in Texas. After finishing the Mount Rushmore job, Lincoln was named park superintendent at the site and went into ranching nearby. But Texas attracted him as it had his father. His wife,

Louella Jones, was a native of Beeville, Texas, so this—and the severe northern winters—decided things.

Lincoln first operated a 900 acre ranch near Beeville in 1944, where he experimented a good deal with soil additives and new grasses. An artist in his own right, he completed many a commission in Texas and also became a photographer. In later years he moved his studio to Harlingen. His recommendation that a museum be created at Mount Rushmore with its story carved in stone suggests very valid questions.

Will anyone remember whose those giant faces are in perhaps 5,000 years or more? Will the story of the United States be recalled? Perhaps the 60 foot heads will be regarded like the carvings of Easter Island. Does that matter? Gutzon and Lincoln Borglum created works of art that perhaps will, like Egyptian sculpture, literally outlive memory.

X.
Afterword

Today, Texas is host to a contingent of pilots from Denmark who occasionally train in the practically year-round favorable flying weather around San Antonio. Danish imports are up and there are a few immigrants entering a variety of occupations across the state, from farming to business.

In recent years, Texas Danes, mostly second and third generation descendants, have made visits to Denmark. The most popular occasion is the Fourth of July celebration in Rebild National Park in Jylland, which attracts thousands, including many Danish Americans. So close are Danish American ties that this celebration is probably the largest "Fourth" celebration outside of the continental United States.

Today, of course, Denmark itself is not the same as when the first emigrants left. The "old country" is a thing of the past. Texas Danes are not the same either. There is a pride in the heritage, but Texas Danes are now—most often—Texans.

Danish group going for an outing

Acknowledgements

The real acknowledgment for a book such as this is the source list. Without former printed works, collections in archives, patient and thorough library staffs, personal interviews and people willing to loan their scrapbooks, it could not have been done.

Special thanks, however, must go to those who helped with a large percentage of the work and who were kind enough to read the entire manuscript.

Harold and Ella Hansen of Danevang were always cooperative and very friendly to me—an "outsider" who showed up years ago wanting Danish Texan information. Theirs was the first home I entered when starting this project one wintry day. I found not only reliable data and a fine collection of local artifacts but also the best coffee cake—served with hot, black coffee—I have ever had.

Mr. and Mrs. Verner Petersen of Danevang have been especially helpful over the years in making photographs and information available. The writings of Verner Petersen's father, P. J. Agerskov Petersen, are still the best source of material on Danevang. Much of this has been translated, and saved with other information, by Mr. Petersen.

Anders Saustrup of Austin has labored unfailingly and willingly, not to say unflinchingly at times, as a translator for much of the material available only in Danish. On occasion, he has suffered through poor handwriting and faint copies to recover a fact. Any errors that remain, and the liberties taken with the Danish poetry, are entirely my own.

The above people were readers of the manuscript along with Mrs. Myrtle Westerfeldt, teacher and descendant of Gillespie County Danes; Leo Westerfeldt, businessman and a Danevang descendant; Mrs. Dorothy Gammel Bohlender, herself an author of a biography of her father, H. P. N. Gammel; Jens Normann Jørgensen of the University of Copenhagen; and Rev. Erik Moller, former pastor at Danevang.

Great appreciation for their support to this project goes to His Excellency Otto Rose Borch, Ambassador of Denmark to the United States, and to Niels Toft, Cultural Counselor of the Royal Danish Embassy, Washington, D.C.

Special thanks go also to Dr. Kristian Hvidt, Danish Parliamentary Librarian, Copenhagen, for making photographs available; to Mrs. Julius Hansen of Happy, Texas, for dealing at length with the Sorrenson photographs and making them available; and to Mrs. Inger Bladt of the Udvandrerarkiv in Aalborg who made archival material available by mail—always a very trying experience.

Encouragements are harder to acknowledge. They came from everyone, none perhaps more welcome than from the man who from the disadvantage of a hospital bed, took my hand and told me he was looking forward to seeing the book. He was a Danish Texan and proud of it. "We're a solid bunch," he said, and smiled for a moment.

—J. L. D.

Photographic Credits

All prints are from the collections of The University of Texas Institute of Texan Cultures at San Antonio, courtesy of the following lenders. Credits from left to right are separated by semicolons and from top to bottom by dashes. Uncredited photographs are staff productions of The University of Texas Institute of Texan Cultures at San Antonio.

Page 9 *Le Tour du Monde*, 1862 (Volume 1, page 88); *Le Tour du Monde*, 1862 (Volume 1, page 113)

Page 10 *Harper's Weekly*, March 5, 1864, page 148

Page 11 John Frost, *Pictorial History of Mexico and the Mexican War*, page 186; *Gleason's Pictorial Drawingroom Companion—Frank Leslie's Illustrated Newspaper*, December 5, 1863, page 173

Page 18 *Frank Leslie's Illustrated Newspaper*, September 16, 1882, page 49; *Illustrated London News*, April 13, 1844

Page 19 Mr. & Mrs. Edwin Trube, Galveston; Institute of Texan Cultures; Mattie Trube Houston

Page 20 Institute of Texan Cultures—Mr. and Mrs. Edwin Trube, Galveston; Mr. and Mrs. Edwin Trube, Galveston

Page 21 *Frank Leslie's Illustrated Newspaper*, September 5, 1863, page 373; *Harper's Weekly*, May 10, 1873, page 393. Drawing by F. O. C. Darley

Page 23 Thomas B. Thorpe, *"Our Army" on the Rio Grande 1846*, page 14; *Frank Leslie's Illustrated Newspaper*, January 24, 1863, page 280—*Frank Leslie's Illustrated Newspaper*, February 7, 1863, page 312; *Harper's Weekly*, January 31, 1863, page 72—S. C. Griffin, *History of Galveston, Texas*

Page 26 *Harper's Weekly*, June 3, 1871, page 509; *Frank Leslie's Illustrated Newspaper*, May 1, 1880, page 140

Page 30 *Harper's Weekly*, November 7, 1894, page 916; *Harper's Weekly*, March 27, 1869, page 204—Edward A. Steiner, *On the Trail of the Immigrant*, facing page 10; *Harper's Weekly*, January 24, 1874, page 76—*Le Tour du Monde*, 1861 (Volume 1, page 253); *Harper's Weekly*, November 13, 1886, page 728. Drawing by R. F. Zogbaum

Page 35 Politikens forlag, Copenhagen

Page 37 Institute of Texan Cultures—Kilman Studio, Fredericksburg; Mrs. Myrtle Westerfeldt, Fredericksburg—Mrs. Stella Jung Browning and Mrs. Myrtle Westerfeldt, Fredericksburg; Mrs. A. O. Kneese and Mrs. Myrtle Westerfeldt, Fredericksburg

Sources

I. The Danish Texans

Zanco
Looscan, Adele B. "Harris County, 1822-1845." *Southwestern Historical Quarterly*, XVIII, (October 1914, 195 f.; January 1915, 261 f.; April 1915, 399 f.).

Williams, Amelia. "A Critical Study of the Siege of the Alamo and of the Personnel of its Defenders." *Southwestern Historical Quarterly*, XXXVII, (Chapter V, April 1934), no. 4.

Hillebrandt
Block, W. T. "Christian Hillebrandt, Cattle Baron." Ms. read before the East Texas Historical and Genealogical Society, in possession of author; personal correspondence.

II. The Start of Emigration

general
Butlin, F. M. *Among the Danes*. N. Y.: James Pott & Co., 1909.

Danstrup, John. *A History of Denmark*. Copenhagen: Wivels Forlag, 1949.

Encyclopedia Britannica. "Denmark." (var. eds.).

Historical Statistics of the United States. U.S. Department of Commerce. Washington: U.S. Printing Office, 1960.

Hvidt, Kristian. *Danes Go West*. Rebild National Park Society, Inc., 1976.

Hvidt, Kristian. *Flight to America*. N. Y.: Academic Press, 1975.

Wattenberg, Ben J. *The Statistical History of the United States.* N. Y.: Basic Books, Inc., 1976.

Aarhus voyage	"Det første Udvandrerskib under dansk Flag til USA afgik fra Aarhus." *Aarhus Stiftstidende,* 17 October 1957.
	Hvidt, Kristian. *Danes Go West.* op. cit.
	"Sørgelig udvandrerfaerd begyndte med annonce." *Aarhus Stiftstidende,* 18 March 1957.
Captain Johnson	Johnson, Peter A. "Two Sea-Captains Johnson and some of their friends." Ms. edited and annotated, unpub., by Hobart Huson (at DRT Library, San Antonio).
Henrichson	Crofford, Lena H. *Pioneers on the Nueces.* San Antonio: The Naylor Co., (1963).

III. A Few Individuals

census	U. S. Census: 1850, 1860.
Trube family	Adams, Don. "Island Family to Abandon Historic Home." *Galveston News,* 25 July 1965 (A, 9).
	Bunjes, Emil. "The Trube House, Galveston." *Port of Galveston.* March 1971, p. 14.
	Coombs, Helen. "Trube Design Said to be 'Exuberant.'" *Galveston Daily News,* 10 September 1967 (B, 19).
	Criswell, Ann Minick. "From the Trubes to Texas." *Galveston News,* 20 April 1966 (1).
	"Recent Marker Given Trube House." *Galveston News,* 11 August 1965 (D, 5).

Trube, Edwin A. Personal correspondence (Galveston).

"Trube Home Featured by Garden Club." *Galveston Island Mirror,* 8 March 1968, p. 4.

Trube, Mrs. Mattie E. Personal correspondence and personal clipping collection (Houston).

Dorbrandt   Debo, Darrell. "Then . . . and Now; Pioneers: The Dorbrandts." *The Burnet Bulletin,* 7 March 1974.

Lovenskiold   deGarmo, Mrs. Frank. *Pathfinders of Texas.* Austin: Von Boeckmann-Jones, Co., 1951.

The Lone Star State, History of Texas. Chicago: Lewis Publishing Co., 1893, pp. 623-624.

McCampbell, Coleman. *Texas Seaport.* N. Y.: Exposition Press (1952). p. 250.

IV. Lee County: "Little Denmark"

Lee Co. colony   "Danish Immigrants' Children Recall Early Lee County Life." Houston *Chronicle,* 28 July 1963.

Killen, Mrs. James C., ed. *History of Lee County, Texas.* Lee County Historical Survey Committee, Quanah: Nortex Press, 1974.

Killen, Mrs. James C. Personal correspondence and interview.

Ramsey, Grover. ms. field notes taken in 1967.

Thomas, Mrs. Adell Sorenson. "Little Danish settlement eight miles west of Lexington." *The Lexington Enterprise,* 20 April 1978.

Thompson, Flora. "The Danes of North Lee County." *Lee County News.* 28 July 1966.

V. Increased Emigration: Individuals and Groups

1870-1890
emigration

Bille, John H. *A History of the Danes in America.* (A reprint from the *Transactions* of the Wisconsin Academy of Sciences, Arts, and Letters, Vol. XI, March 1896) San Francisco: R and E Research Associates. 1971.

Brown, Francis J. and Joseph S. Roucek, eds. *One America.* Englewood Cliffs, N. J.: Prentice-Hall, Inc., 1945

Ferenczi, Imre. "A Historical Study of Migration Statistics." *International Labour Review:* II (1929), pp. 356-384.

Friis, Erik J., ed. *The Scandinavian Presence in North America.* N. Y.: Harper's Magazine Press, 1973.

Hvidt, Kristian. "Danish Emigration Prior to 1914, Trends and Problems." *Scandinavian Economic Review:* 14:158-178.

Nielsen, Alfred C. *Life in an American Denmark.* Des Moines, Iowa: (n.p.), 1962.

Skaardal, Dorothy Burton. *The Divided Heart* (Scandinavian Immigrant Experience Through Literary Sources). Oslo: Universitetsforlaget, (1974). Also: Lincoln: University of Nebraska Press.

Willcox, Walter F., ed. *International Migrations.* Intro. and notes by Imre Ferenczi. Geneva, N. Y.: National Bureau of Economic Research, International Labour Office. (Vol. 1) 1929; (Vol. 2) 1931. See, Chapter XI, "Migration Statistics of Denmark, Norway and Sweden," by Adolph Jensen.

Captain Peetz

History of Texas, Together With a Biographical History of the Cities of Houston and Galveston, Containing a Concise History of the State . . . Chicago: Lewis Publishing Co., 1895, pp. 705-706.

Andersen

Wallace, Laura Andersen. "Christian Andersen," *One Hundred Years in Bandera.* J. Marvin Hunter, ed., n.p. 1953.

Sorensen, Petersen

Hunter, J. Marvin, ed. *One Hundred Years in Bandera.* n.p., 1953.

Rasmussen

"Automobile firm name is changed." *Galveston Tribune,* January 2, 1931, p. 16, col. 5.

Graham, Samuel Butler, ed. *Galveston Community Book.* Galveston, Texas: Arthur H. Cawston, 1945. pp. 385-387.

Griffin, S. C. *A History of Galveston, Texas: Narrative and Biographical.* Galveston: A. H. Cawston, 1931. p. 265.

"Island Ford agency sold to Coffman." *Galveston Daily News.* May 13, 1964, p. 13.

"Isle Ford Dealers Consolidate; Ken Ward joins Rasmussen firm." *Galveston Daily News.* May 27, 1932, p. 16, col. 6.

"Obituary." *Galveston Daily News,* March 23, 1946, p. 2.

"Rasmussen buys control in firm." *Galveston Daily News,* November 15, 1930.

Sorenson, J.

Padclock, Buckley B. *A Twentieth Century History and Biographical Record of North and West Texas.* Chicago and N. Y.: The Lewis Publishing Company, 1906.

107

Striegler family	Gillespie County Historical Society. *Pioneers in God's Hills*. Austin: Von Boeckmann Jones, Vol. 1, 1960, Vol. 2, 1974.
	Striegler Family History. (Fredericksburg).
Bader	S. W. Pease Collection, ITC: *Express*, 22 October 1908 and *Light*, October 1908.
Mathisen	*Fredericksburg Standard*, 29 October 1975.
	Personal files and interview: Mrs. Myrtle Westerfeldt, Fredericksburg.
Gammel	Bohlender, Dorothy Gammel. Personal correspondence and interview.
	Bohlender, Dorothy Gammel and Frances Tarlton McCallum. "H. P. N. Gammel, Texas Bookman," unpub. ms. in possession of authors.
	"Firemen Fight in Vain to Save First Capitol and Contents." *Austin Statesman* reprint with additions on 26 July 1970 of "The State's Calamity," from the *Statesman* of 10 November 1881.
	Smithwick, Noah. *Evolution of a State*. Intro. by James M. Day. Austin: Steck-Vaughan Co., (facsm.) 1968.
	"Texas Collection." *Southwestern Historical Quarterly*, Vol. 45, (October 1941), pp. 192-193.
	The University of Texas at Austin, Archives: vertical files.
	The University of Texas at Austin, Barker Texas History Center: Gammel file (ms. of Nellie Gammel Kingdom, 1931).

Winkler, E. W. "Gammel." *The Handbook of Texas*, Vol. 1., Ed. Walter Prescott Webb, 1952.

VI. Danevang: the Danish Field

Christensen, Thomas P. "Danevang, Texas." *Southwestern Historical Quarterly*, XXXII, (July 1928), pp. 67-73.

County Records: Wharton County Clerk's Office.

Danevang Community Anniversary, 1894-1944. n.p., n.d. (1944). (P.J. Agerskov Petersen, ed.)

Danevang Community Anniversary, 1894-1944 n.p., n.d. (1976). (Translation of the 1944 publication's Danish sections, Verner A. Petersen and Mrs. Michael Plentl, eds.)

"Danevang—Community of Co-Ops." *Texas Co-Op Power*, February 1964.

"Danevang School." *El Campo Citizen*, 19 October 1957.

"Danevang, Texas." (Ms. in collection of Verner A. Petersen, Danevang).

Danske i Amerika. Minneapolis and Chicago, 1908.

Davis, John L. "Danes Came to Central Wharton County in 1894." *The Bridge.* Journal of the Danish American Heritage Society, May 1978.

Davis, John L. "Danes in Texas." *The Handbook of Texas*, Vol. III, ed. Eldon Stephen Branda, Austin: Texas State Historical Association, 1976.

Den Danske Evangelisk-Lutherske Kirke i Amerika, 1871-1921. Cedar Falls, Iowa: 1921.

Den danske Kvindeforening records and taped interviews, final meeting, Danevang, April 1971.

Flachmeier, William A. *Lutherans of Texas in Confluence,* n.p., n.d.

Franke, Paul. "Foreign Flavor of Texas." *Houston Chronicle Magazine,* 14 December 1947.

Grand View College, Des Moines, Iowa, Library Archives.

Grantham, Grace Cone. "The Danes in Wharton County," MA Thesis, Texas College of Arts and Industry, Kingsville, August 1947.

Henningsen, L. ed. *Danske Folkesamfunds Jubileaumshaefte 1887-1912.* pp. 25-28.

Hermansen, H. P. "Danevang, Texas." *Jule Granen.* December 1908. Tr. by Verner A. Petersen (Ms. in his possession, Danevang).

Holley, James O. "Danevang Is Only Danish Community." *Houston Post,* 25 October 1953.

Holub, Veronica. "Another Danish Christmas." *El Campo Leader-News,* 22 December 1976.

Hunt, Herschiel. "Danevang Bicentennial Program Set." *El Campo Leader-News,* 2 June 1976.

(Interviews at Danevang listed in section IV: prominent ones are Pastor Moller, Mrs. Elizabeth Juhl, Verner Petersen, Harold and Ella Hansen, Mr. and Mrs. Carl Hansen, Mrs. Wilbur Webb, Carl Hansen Sr.)

Jensen, Mrs. Hans O. "Give Me a Flower While I
Live." (Ms. in possession of Verner A.
Petersen, Danevang).

Koock, Mary Faulk. "A Texas Velkommen." *The
Texas Star,* 10 December 1972.

Lund, F. P. J. "Life Among Danish Settlers in
Texas." Translation of and ms. in possession
of Verner A. Petersen, Danevang.

Nyholm, Paul C. *The Americanization of the
Danish Lutheran Churches in America.*
Copenhagen & Minneapolis, 1963.

Pedersen, John. "Tribute to Agerskov Petersen."
Lutheran Tidings, February 20, 1958, p. 11.

Petersen, Dennis. "Danevang." *The Junior
Historian.* January 1967, Vol. 27, No. 4 (p. 21,
22, 28).

Petersen, Mrs. Earl. "Danevang Community
Began in Denmark in Late 19th Century." *El
Campo Citizen,* 7 and 14 May 1968.

Petersen, Mrs. Earl. Personal correspondence,
interviews.

Petersen, P. J. Agerskov. "A Brief History of St.
Ansgar's Congregation, Danevang, Texas."
and "Postscript." (Tr. by Michael Mikkelsen,
Ms. in collection of Verner A. Petersen,
Danevang).

Petersen, P. J. Agerskov. "Danevang, Wharton
County, Texas." (Ms. tr. by Peter Harton, in
collection of Verner A. Petersen, Danevang).

Petersen, P. J. Agerskov. "James P. Olson."
Dannevirke, December 28, 1928. Tr. by Verner
A. Petersen (Ms. in his possession, Danevang).

Strandskov, Holger. "P. J. Agerskov-Petersen."
  Kirke og Folk (November, 1958). (Tr. by Verner
  A. Petersen).

Williams, Annie Lee. *A History of Wharton
  County, 1846-1961.* Austin, Texas, 1964.

VII. A New Century

later settlers   Brown, et al., eds. *One America.* op. cit.

    Hvidt, "Danish Emigration Prior to 1914 . . ."
      op. cit.

emigration   *Abstracts of Reports of the Immigration
      Commission* (var.).

    Ferenczi, "A Historical Study . . ." op. cit.

    Friis. *Scandinavian Presence in North
      America.* op. cit.

    Krontoff, Torben. "Factors in Assimilation: A
      Comparative Study." *Norwegian-American
      Studies,* Vol. 26. Norwegian-American
      Historical Association, Northfield, Minnesota,
      1974.

    Skaardal, *The Divided Heart.* op. cit.

    Willcox-Ferenczi, *International Migrations.*
      op. cit.

Kohler   Mrs. Dagmar Cole, Hebbronville, interview.

    Ramsey, Grover. Ms. field notes taken in 1968.

    Wharton, Clarence Ray. *Texas Under Many
      Flags.* Chicago and N. Y.: The American
      Historical Society, Inc., Vol. 5, p. 35.

Kristoffersen   *Art and Artists of Texas*, p. 140.

Ingwersen   "C. T. Ingwersen, Age 68, Is Dead." Beaumont
                       Enterprise, 1 November 1930.

Jensen   Peterman, V. M. Ms. in personal possession (and
                       in files of Lamb County Historical Committee,
                       Littlefield, Texas).

Guldmann   "Guldmann services to be held today." *Galveston
                       Daily News*, 3 August 1932, (p. 8).

                       "Guldmann Services Today." *Galveston Tribune*,
                       3 August 1932 (p. 8).

                       "Hans Guldmann Found Shot to Death in
                       Bathroom of Home Here." *Galveston Tribune*,
                       1 August 1932 (p. 1).

Christensen   "Christensen Farm." *Galveston Daily News*,
                       13 January 1929, p. 4, col. 2.

Rasmussen   "Christensen Farm in County: Unlimited Variety
                       of Products Suitable to Soil." *Galveston Daily
                       News*, 1 October 1928, p. 19C, col. 5.

                       Davis, Ellis and Edwin H. Grobe, eds. *The New
                       Encyclopedia of Texas*. Dallas: Texas
                       Development Bureau, n.d. (Vol. 1, p. 96).

                       Griffin, op. cit.

                       Graham, op. cit.

                       In the Rosenberg Library vertical files, the
                       clippings on Rasmussen have their titles cut
                       away, but articles are: *Galveston Tribune*, 2
                       January 1931, p. 16 and *Galveston News*, 23
                       March 1946. p. 2.

                       "John Christensen." *Galveston News*, 5
                       November 1930.

"John Christensen Claimed By Death." *Galveston Daily News,* 15 December 1934 (p. 1).

Amsterdam-Liverpool   Ramsey, Grover. ms. field notes, 1969.

general   Krist, Anton, ed. *Jubilee and World's Fair Yearbook.* Danish National Committee, Chicago, 1933.

Mortensen, Enok. *Danish-American Life and Letters, A Bibliography.* The Committee on Publications of the Danish Evangelical Lutheran Church in America. Des Moines, Iowa: Grand View College, 1945.

Sorrenson   Hansen, Mrs. Doris. "The H. W. Sorrenson Family" and "Henry William Sorrenson" Mss. in author's possession (Happy, Texas); personal correspondence and interviews.

Bentsen family   "Bentsen Likes to Get Things Done." *Houston Post,* 3 June 1962.

Bentsen, Lloyd M. Jr. "Critical Water Problems Demand Unified Teamwork." *South Texan.*

Bentsen vertical files in Barker Texas History Center, University of Texas at Austin.

"Firm Hits Snags in '40's." *Dallas Morning News,* 30 September 1974.

Lloyd Bentsen Sr. Personal interview.

M. I. "Winning and losing with LBJr." *The Texas Observer,* 14 March 1975.

McNeely, Dave. "Elder Bentsen Unhappy Doing Nothing." *Dallas Morning News,* 30 September 1974.

R. D. "Lloyd Bentsen's Fortune." *The Texas Observer,* 3 and 17 April 1970.

"Top Challenger to Yarborough Prefers Middle."
Dallas Herald, 9 October 1963.

Watson, Mrs. James. *The Lower Rio Grande Valley of Texas, and Its Builders*. San Antonio, 1931.

Kristenstad

Ficklen, Mary. "Texas' Lost Utopia." *Texas Parade*, May 1971.

Hammond, C. M. "Kristenstad: A Practical Utopia." *The Texas Weekly*, 29 August 1931.

Landon, Frances O. and Verdi MacLennan. "Kristenstad, a Novel Colony on the Brazos." *Dallas Morning News*, 22 January 1933, (Features Section, p. 3).

Nunn, W. C. *Somervell, Story of a Texas County*. Ft. Worth: Texas Christian University Press, 1975.

Ramsey, Grover and John L. Davis. Ms. field notes, 1968-1970.

Shuffler, R. Henderson, Ms. personal files.

VIII. "Is There Nothing Left from the Good Old Days?

Danevang

See references to section VI.

travel comments

Andersen, Georg. *Dette forbløffende Amerika*. Aarhus: Forlaget Aros, 1949.

Clauson-Kaas, Knud. *Vi ruller gennem Amerika*. Kobenhavn: Casper Nielsens Forlag, 1948.

IX. Recent Emigration

Daugbjerg

"Former Consul." *Houston Chronicle*, 19 June 1971.

Mulvany, Tom. "Dane's Demanding Post." *Houston Chronicle*, 24 November 1968.

Borglums   Acheson, Sam. "Texas Irresistibly Attracted Borglum." *Dallas News*, 7 March 1941.

"Borglum Dies, Son to Finish Masterpiece." n.p., n.d., clipping file, Barker Texas History Center, University of Texas at Austin.

"Famed Sculptor Does Memorial to 3 Texans." Austin *American-Statesman*, 10 August 1955.

Jayson, Sharon. "Mount Rushmore Sculptor, Lincoln Borglum." *Southwest Airlines Magazine*, September 1978, pp. 59-63.

McGahey, Fred. "A Tale of Two Borglums." *San Antonio Express Magazine*, 21 Sept. 1952.

"Nation's Birthday a Flop." Austin *American-Statesman*, 2 July 1976.

Price, Willadene. *Gutzon Borglum*. Chicago: Rand McNally & Co., 1961.

"Texas Sculptor Dated by Women's Federation." Austin *American-Statesman*, 13 Feb. 1955.

Wedemeyer, Henry. "Gutzon Borglum." *The Pioneer*, October 1925. (p. 2-3, 29).

general   *Denmark* (Naval Intelligence Division of the Admiralty, Great Britain) Geographical Handbook Series. January 1944. University Press, Cambridge: H. M. Stationery Office (1944).

Denmark, An Official Handbook. Press and Information Department, Royal Danish Ministry of Foreign Affairs, Christiansborg Palace, Copenhagen, 1970.

INTERVIEWS, PERSONAL CORRESPONDENCE, MANUSCRIPT MATERIAL
PRIVATELY HELD

Mrs. Eleanor R. Austin, LaMarque
Mary Fay Barnes, Galveston Historical Commission
Rudy Bendixen, San Benito
Dr. Maurice Boyd, Chairman, Department of History, Texas Christian
    University, Ft. Worth
Dr. Keith L. Bryant, Head, Department of History, Texas A&M University,
    College Station
Mrs. Bill Bryson, Chairman, Burnet County Historical Commission
Dora Christensen, Elgin
Mrs. James G. Cole, Hebbronville
Den danske Kvindeforening members: Abelone Harton, Agnes Jensen,
    Emil Svensson, Agnes Hansen, Anna Lykke, Ida Thyssen,
    Mary Andersen, Anna Nelsen, Carl Thyssen, Elizabeth Juhl,
    Marie Thyssen (The men are husbands . . .), Danevang
Ealy Dorbrandt, Ballard Dorbrandt, Mrs. Lillian Sawyer, Burnet
Dr. Catherine Drew, Chairman, Department of History, Rice University,
    Houston
Mrs. Doris Gray, Sugarland
Dr. Thomas C. Greaves, Director, Division of Social Science, The University
    of Texas at San Antonio
Miss Marguerite Haggard, Plano
Mrs. R. L. Halvorsen, LaMarque
Mr. and Mrs. Carl Hansen Sr., Danevang
Hansen Collection, Harold and Ella Hansen, Danevang
Mrs. Julius Hansen, Happy
Walter Hansen, Clifton
Mrs. O. L. Harton, Danevang
Paul D. Hedemann, Consul, Royal Danish Consulate, Houston
Jack Holzhueter, State Historical Society of Wisconsin, Madison
Dr. Kristian Hvidt, Copenhagen
Mrs. Elizabeth Juhl, Danevang
Preston Ilseng, Huffman
Dr. John King, Chairman, Department of History, University of Houston
Dr. Johannes Knudsen, Des Moines (*Kirke og Folk*, Secretary)
Mrs. Trevor C. Lucey, Galveston
Mrs. Marius Madsen, McAllen
Charles Curtis Mahavier Jr., Liberty
Fred Mathisen, Fredericksburg
Myreta Matthews, Williamson County Historical Commission, Liberty Hill

John A. McDonald, Wichita Falls
Pastor Erik Moller, Danevang
J. P. Nielsen, Falfurrias
Thomas A. Paulson, Falls
Mrs. L. W. Pearson, Arcadia
Mrs. Earl Petersen, Danevang
P. J. Agerskov Petersen Collection, Mr. and Mrs. Verner A. Petersen,
    Danevang
Mrs. Tom Peterson, Hutto
Sandra Pickett, Chairman, Liberty County Historical Commission, Liberty
Elizabeth R. Pink, Chairman, Cullen County Historical Commission, Frisco
Professor Robert L. Reid, Administrative Chairman, Department of History,
    Baylor University, Waco
Mrs. Albert Richter, Taylor
Mrs. Omar Robinson, Meridian
Anders Saustrup, Austin
Calra Stearns Scarbrough, Georgetown
Dr. Kenneth V. Shover, Chairman, Department of History, The University of
    Texas at El Paso
Cecil Striegler, Brady
Dr. David M. Vigness, Chairperson, Department of History, Texas Tech
    University, Lubbock
Mrs. Wilbur Webb Jr., Danevang
Mrs. Myrtle Westerfeldt, Fredericksburg
Dr. Hal Williamson, Chairman, Department of History, Southern Methodist
    University, Dallas
Dr. Joseph Wilson, Department of German, Rice University, Houston
Lucille Wilson, Grosbeck
Mrs. J. B. Wyley, Hutto

PUBLIC AND PROFESSIONAL ARCHIVES

Dana College, Archives, Blair, Nebraska
The Danish American Heritage Society, Junction City, Oregon
The Danish Brotherhood in America, Omaha, Nebraska
Grand View College, Archives, Des Moines, Iowa
Racine County Historical Museum, Racine, Wisconsin (Hist. Assn.)
The Rosenberg Library, Galveston, Texas
Royal Danish Embassy, Washington, and Consulate in Houston, Texas
State Archives, Austin, Texas
The Texas Collection, Baylor University, Waco, Texas
Udvandrerarkivet (Danes Worldwide Archives), Aalborg, Denmark

The University of Texas at Austin, Archives and Barker Texas History Center
Wharton County Junior College (Hansen Memorial Coll.), Wharton, Texas

Teachers and students can go to any large library to get general Danish material. The locations listed here are probably the most useful.

CURRENT PERIODICALS

American Dane Magazine
Bien
The Bridge, Journal of the Danish American Heritage Society
Danish Foreign Office Journal
Den Danske Pioneer
Kirke og Folk

INDEX

Page numbers refer to major references. Italic numerals identify photographs.